How My Faith Brought Me Through From Diagnosis to Loss: Heartbreak to Healing

Nicole Estelle Roman

Chosen Pen Publishing

Fayetteville, NC

Copyright © 2024 by Dr. Nicole Roman

Except as provided by the Copyright Act, no part of this publication may be reproduced, stored in a retrieval system, or transmitted in any form or by any means without the prior written permission of the publisher. Permission requests should be requested in writing to The Chosen Pen, 1420 Hoke Loop Road, Fayetteville, NC 28314.

Scripture quotations are taken from The Holy Bible King James Version unless otherwise specified.
The Holy Bible, English Standard Version. ESV® Text Edition: 2016. Copyright © 2001 by Crossway Bibles, a publishing ministry of Good News Publishers.
Holy Bible, New International Version, Copyright© 1973, 1978, 1984 by International Bible Society.

This book is for informational purposes only, even if and regardless of whether it features the advice of physicians and medical practitioners. This book is not, nor is it intended to be, a substitute for professional medical advice, diagnosis, or treatment and should never be relied upon for specific medical advice. The views expressed in this book are the views of the expert and do not necessarily represent the views of Chosen Pen.

ISBN-978-1-952315-21-3
Library of Congress Control Number:
Cover & Book Interior by The Ready Write-Her

How My Faith Brought Me Through From Diagnosis to Loss: Heartbreak to Healing /Dr. Nicole Estelle Roman
1. Non-Fiction-Spiritual and Religion
2. Non-Fiction-Self-Help
3. Non-Fiction-Grief

To order additional copies of the resource, please send requests to:
Dr. Nicole Roman
PO Box 465781
Lawrenceville, GA 30042
Website: realnicoleestelle.com

Printed in the United States of America
10 9 8 7 6 5 4 3 2 1

- To the enduring legacy of My Daughter, Sophia Nicole Roman, who in her three short years, imparted profound lessons of love, faith, compassion, mercy, and kindness. Through her innocent and gentle spirit, she illuminated the path towards living life to the fullest, regardless of the challenges we face.

- For all the unsung little warriors – the courageous souls who lost the fight and those who are still engaged in the relentless battle against cancer. To those brave fighters who uphold the banner of faith, confronting the beast with unwavering resolve. And to their caregivers, whose unwavering support serves as a beacon of hope in the darkest of times.

- In memory of Sophia Nicole and in solidarity with all those touched by the struggles of illness, may this book serve as a testament to the enduring power of love, faith, hope, and the human spirit.

Sophia Nicole

r}-wh,t, 6/ 2008 - r}-,,,_.n.e, 2] ; 2611

CONTENTS

Introduction	1
Chapter 1: The Fairytale	7
Chapter 2: Diagnosis	17
Chapter 3: Burden Lifter	27
Chapter 4: Treatment Phase 1	31
Chapter 5: It's Pouring	37
Chapter 6: Treatment - Advancing Forward	43
Chapter 7: Treatment Escalates	69
Chapter 8: Battling The Beast	119
Chapter 9: Resurgence	145
Chapter 10: Goodbye	165
Chapter 11: After The Ground Settles	173
Chapter 12: Therapy's Impact	191
Chapter 13: God's Time	195
Chapter 14: Beauty From Ashes	201
Chapter 15: Hope Lives	205
Chapter 16: The Gift of Prayer	213
Acknowledgements	221
About the Author	227

INTRODUCTION

Before my daughter's birth, the sight of a St. Jude commercial prompted me to change the channel instinctively. Witnessing children in pain was too much to bear. Little did I know that those heart-wrenching scenes would later become my reality during my daughter's life journey. As hospital visits became less frequent and calls dwindled, my husband and I found ourselves increasingly isolated in our struggle, feeling utterly alone. We longed for support, for someone to hold our hand and guide us through the darkest and most terrifying time of our lives. Despite our roles as servant leaders, seeking comfort from fellow believers in our church community, we discovered that no one could truly relate to our journey. No one was able to show us how to carry this heavy burden while maintaining our faith as we moved forward.

Truth be told, the church we were part of at the time was ill-equipped to minister to us. Indeed, I believe God can minister through His Spirit. However, no one there had experienced a similar trial and the pastor had not fostered a healthy, selfless environment. It was only years after our daughter's passing that God led us to a church where true healing was nurtured.

The inspiration for this book arose from the profound need for support that we ourselves did not receive. When my daughter passed at three years old, I felt as if I was suffocating, desperately grasping for anything to help me navigate through the overwhelming pain. In those moments of anguish and despair, I turned to books, blogs, and support groups in search of comfort and guidance. Yet, amidst the multitude of resources, I found a void—an absence of the specific kind of support and understanding that could only come from walking a similar path of faith and struggle. This book is born from that void, from the longing for connection and shared experience amidst the turmoil of grief. It is a testament to the unwavering resilience of the human spirit and the sustaining power of faith in the face of adversity.

HOW MY FAITH BROUGHT ME THROUGH

To embark on this emotional journey alongside me, it is vital to understand one fundamental truth: I am deeply rooted in my faith as a woman of God, and it intricately intertwines with every aspect of this narrative. As you immerse yourself in the chapters of my shared testimony—the diagnosis, the treatment, and the loss of our beloved daughter—you will discover that the path to healing is open to us all. As I journey through grief towards restoration, you will come to realize that my connection with God is not just a mere facet of my character; it is the very cornerstone upon which I see and navigate through life. I acknowledge that every reader brings their own set of beliefs and perspectives. You are encouraged to engage with this testimony and glean lessons, insights, and inspiration according to your understanding. As a Christian, my role is not to impose my beliefs upon you, but rather to express God's love, His Word, and my personal experiences with Him. I offer this disclaimer to foster an environment where you can freely explore God's love from a different lens.

I invite you to journey alongside me, witnessing the highs and lows, the tribulations, and triumphs, with the understanding that within these pages lies something that will speak to your heart.

It has taken twelve years to gather the courage to write this testimony. This book could only be penned from a place of healing, to allow my heart the ability to revisit some of the most painfully dark moments of my life.

As you turn the pages, my prayer is that it will activate healing within your own heart. May you see how you too can apply your faith to move forward, knowing that you have a race to finish! Join me on this journey—a journey from sickness to healing, from despair to hope, and, from grief to restoration.

As we begin, let us pause for a moment to pray as we are, guided by the light of God's love, with the assurance that we will reach the other side!

Heavenly Father,

As readers embark on this emotional journey, You see each heartache, every struggle, and every longing for healing. Just as it is written in Psalms 34:17-18, "The righteous cry out, and the LORD hears them; He delivers them from all their troubles. The LORD is close to the brokenhearted and saves those who are crushed in spirit."

Lord, you understand the complexities of our suffering and the need for healing that resides within each soul. I ask that You touch the hearts of every reader, bringing them comfort and peace amid their pain.

Where there is loneliness, may Your presence be felt as a constant companion. Where there is despair, may Your love lift them, guiding them toward hope and restoration. Father, where there is brokenness, may Your love mend the shattered pieces, bringing wholeness and healing. I pray that as each reader engages with this testimony, they will profoundly encounter Your love.

May Your Word speak life into their circumstances, bringing comfort to their hearts and strength to their spirits. May this book serve as a source of inspiration and encouragement, reminding each reader that they are not alone in their struggles. May they find peace in Your promises and hope in Your unfailing love.

In the of name, Jesus, let Your will be done,
Amen.

CHAPTER 1
The Fairytale

As little girls, so many of us are exposed to and captivated by the idea of finding our happily ever after and drawn to the enchanting narratives of fairy tales, where love triumphs over all. Growing up immersed in these tales through books and movies, I also embraced awaiting my own Prince Charming, who would sweep me off my feet. These youthful fantasies carried into my adulthood, where I envisioned a life of perfection, complete with two children, a faithful dog, and the quintessential white picket fence. I believed it so profoundly that I willingly waited for over a decade, refraining from dating and intimacy, placing my trust in God to unveil my prince in His divine timing.

Then, one day, as I cleaned the church bathroom, I saw a man leaving the sanctuary. Since it was after service and I did not recognize him, I wondered if anyone talked to him. I sprung up and went to greet him. His name was Juan, and after two months of coming to my church, we started dating. On our second outing over coffee, we discussed what we would name our future children. Elijah Juan, for a boy, and Sophia Nicole, for a girl. Six months later, we stood together at the altar, exchanging vows and promising to build a life filled with love, faith, and an unwavering commitment until death do us part.

Shortly after our honeymoon, my seven-year-old godson Dom, whom I have adored since I laid eyes on him at three years old, was removed from his home and placed in foster care. It took a year to navigate through classes, travel back and forth from business trips to meet case workers, undergo background checks, endure home visits, and more. Finally, we were able to welcome him to our

HOW MY FAITH BROUGHT ME THROUGH

home. As we settled into this new chapter, fate intervened, and to my surprise, I found out I was pregnant.

After taking the pregnancy test, I found myself seated on the edge of the bed, surrounded by a mixture of excitement and nervous energy. The question persisted: Was I truly prepared for all the responsibilities of caring for a newborn? I never entertained the notion that our precious gift from God would be anything less than perfect or healthy. I believed in my heart since I waited throughout my twenties on God for my husband, that I would live happily ever after in my thirties.

Beautifully, I wrapped the positive pregnancy test and a bib that said, "You're the Best Daddy Ever," and eagerly awaited Juan's return home. The sheer joy on Juan's face, when he saw the positive pregnancy test, is a moment I will cherish forever. Our fairy tale was coming alive with the thrill of building the perfect life and the beautiful family we envisioned.

In the quiet anticipation of our first ultrasound, we chuckled as the baby moved like a jumping bean on the screen. Amidst the fluttering of a tiny heart, the realization dawned upon us – this was not mere wishful thinking; it was truly happening. Our journey was indeed forming into a beautiful story.

As my waistline expanded and the subtle changes in my body became more apparent, I often whispered conversations to my baby about our life together and my hopes and dreams for their future. When the day finally arrived to find out the sex of our baby, it seemed like Christmas, a sneak peek into the gift of our future. Then, the technician said the words Juan wanted to hear, "You're having a girl." Juan lit up like a Christmas tree; after years of spoiling his two nieces, he had always longed for his baby girl. Baby Sophia Nicole was scheduled to arrive in June, a fitting gift as Juan himself is a June baby.

HOW MY FAITH BROUGHT ME THROUGH

As I entered the eighth month of pregnancy, Juan and I began preparing for Sophia's arrival. Since my job assignment was nearly completed, I planned to work until the week before her due date. On my drive home from work one evening, while lost in prayer, my fairytale began to shatter.

I heard God's voice clearly, "As Mary saw Jesus suffer, you too will see your daughter suffer." Those words echoed in my mind as I cried uncontrollably while trembling behind the wheel. It seemed like someone knocked the wind out of me. Immediately, I turned to script writing in my head, grappling with the meaning behind the words I just heard. What did God mean? What kind of suffering awaited Sophia? Considering Jesus did not start his ministry until he was thirty, was this also an indication of Sophia's timing?

Tears still streamed down my cheeks as I stepped through the door, and without delay, I poured out to Juan what I had just heard from God. His response was simple yet profound, "We will pray." As our hearts were in turmoil, there was a strange comfort in the fact that God had not uttered the word "die." It was a detail we did not dare revisit until it became unavoidable. Quietly, we tucked that revelation away in the corners of our minds, our unspoken understanding that whatever lay ahead would not manifest for many years.

I was hesitant to include God's revelation about Sophia's future suffering in this book. It was not because of doubts about whether God communicates with His children but because of a concern that some readers might respond angrily toward God Himself. My hesitation stemmed from a genuine fear that my words could inadvertently widen the gap in someone's heart toward God. Yet, to omit this revelation would feel disingenuous to our testimony, as it became something that loomed over us in the years ahead.

My journey taught me that our anger towards God is often fueled from our flawed perspectives. Our finite understanding struggles to fathom the depths of His love and the intricacies of His plans. While God did not inflict my daughter's illness upon us, He foresaw what lay ahead. In His boundless love, He chose to warn me, not to crush me, but to strengthen me for future challenges.

As Isaiah 55:8-9 reminds us, "For My thoughts are not your thoughts, nor are your ways My ways," says the Lord. For as the heavens are higher than the earth, so are My ways higher than yours, and My thoughts than your thoughts."

HOW MY FAITH BROUGHT ME THROUGH

In such moments, it is crucial to acknowledge that God's intentions surpass our comprehension. Though sometimes shrouded in the pain of our trials, His love remains steadfast. Embracing this truth has been pivotal in releasing the anger in my heart while navigating life's storms, as my faith was challenged consistently.

The Arrival

When I went for my thirty-seven-week ultrasound, the doctor delivered news that caught us completely off guard. He informed us that the fluid around our daughter was dangerously low and advised us to go home, eat, pack, and return to the hospital that evening to have our baby.

The weight of his words settled in, but the shock left us momentarily numb. Since we did not have our baby shower yet, we only possessed a few outfits, onesies, essentials, and a Pack N' Play. After the initial disbelief wore off, Juan swiftly assembled the Pack N' Play while I gathered the necessities for our hospital stay. With anticipation and apprehension, we made our way to the hospital.

The induction began around eight in the evening, with Juan filling the room with soothing worship music as I drifted in and out of sleep. The night passed peacefully until labor pains began to make their presence known around 4:30 am. Then, the gospel group Shekinah Glory's song "Yes" filled the room, coinciding with the intensifying pain. At that moment, I instinctively requested to keep the song on repeat. There was an inexplicable sense that it was the only thing capable of soothing both my spirit and the increasing agony. As the lyrics echoed, "Will your heart and soul say yes? Will your spirit still say yes? There is more that I require of the..." Between the chorus, I heard God say for us to continue playing this song, because it must get into Sophia's spirit. Little did I realize then that we all needed to get a "yes" into our spirits for what lies ahead.

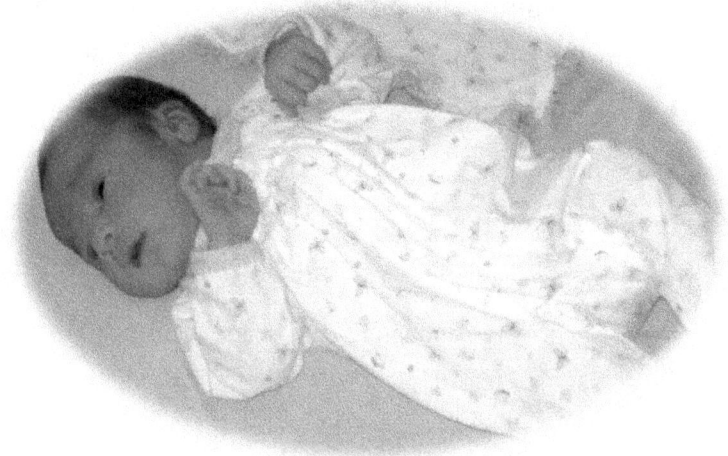

Sophia Nicole entered the world at precisely 5:38 am, her arrival announced by the cries that echoed in the room. It was a moment of pure joy as we looked upon her tiny form with awe and wonder. Juan and I knew that our lives would never be the same again. Once again, God's words rang in my head, "Yes, has to get into Sophia's spirit." All I could think was, why and for what reason?

Sophia & Mommy

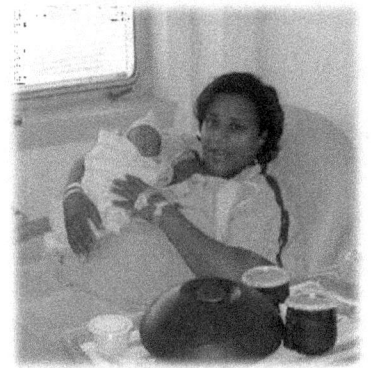

Sophia & Daddy

Sophia & Big Brother

Our Family

CHAPTER 2
Diagnosis

"...He causes his sun to rise on the evil and the good and sends rain on the righteous and the unrighteous."
Matthew 5:45 (NIV)

As we brought Sophia home from the hospital, I found myself compulsively snapping photographs, capturing every smile, every coo, every fleeting expression. It was not something I openly admitted, but deep down, I harbored a quiet fear. I feared that if something happened to Sophia, these photographs would become my only tie to her, my only lifeline to the precious moments we shared.

Everything followed the typical script during the initial months of our baby's life. Yes, there were those moments of intense crying, but we attributed them to her simply being a typical fussy newborn. When Sophia was around three months old, Juan and I noticed something peculiar in her left eye in some of her pictures.

At first, I thought it was just a trick of the camera, oddly capturing her eye. Never did it cross our minds that something serious could be brewing. Sometimes, when the light hit her eye exactly right, I would see what seemed like a clear pupil, only for it to disappear just as quickly. I even playfully nicknamed it "lights on, lights off" because I could not understand it. I searched the internet for answers, but my searches turned up empty-handed because I used the term "clear pupil" instead of "white."

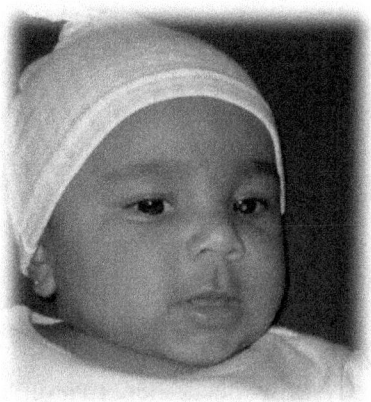

When Sophia turned three months old, we visited her pediatrician for her checkup. I explained to him what I saw occasionally in her pictures. The doctor conducted a thorough examination, shining lights into her eyes to check for any abnormalities. The doctor informed us that he did

HOW MY FAITH BROUGHT ME THROUGH

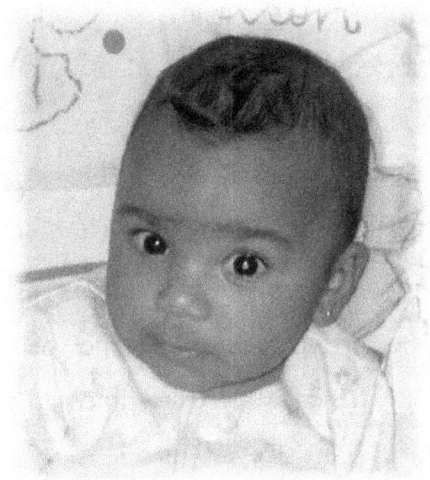

not see anything unusual. However, his news did not take away the uneasy feeling I had in the pit of my stomach. Deep down, I knew something was happening, but it was not the right time for the revelation.

As Sophia grew, I noticed the anomaly more frequently. However, it was not until her pediatric six-month checkup that the issue became apparent. Once again, I mentioned my concerns to her pediatrician. This time, during the eye exam, he seemed visibly alarmed. He wasted no time providing me with the contact information of a specialist in New York and urged me to schedule an immediate appointment. Fear began to tighten its grip on our hearts.

The next day, we rushed to see the eye specialist in New York. His diagnosis sent shock waves through my husband and I - there were many issues affecting Sophia's eyes, and he noted her left eye had a retinal detachment. Without delay, he arranged for us to meet with the Chief of the Ophthalmic Oncology Service at the cancer hospital in New York City. As we hurried to the CANCER hospital, the weight of dread hung heavy around our necks.

Upon our arrival, the world-renowned Chief of the Ophthalmic Department wasted no time and performed an ultrasound on Sophia's eyes in the busy exam room. Visiting doctors who were there to learn from the Chief packed the room. They were all throwing around technical words and asking questions, fascinated by what they saw in our baby's eyes.

It seemed like we had been transported back to high school science class, where we watched the teacher dissect a frog while the rest of the class marveled at the process. But to our horror, it was our baby lying on that cold metal table. Despite our overwhelming fear for our daughter, it seemed nobody noticed or cared as we stood in the corner, desperately trying to hold ourselves together in the unfolding nightmare. In my head, I kept repeating, "Jesus, please help us," feeling like I watched the whole scene from outside my own body.

HOW MY FAITH BROUGHT ME THROUGH

After what felt like an eternity, someone finally ushered us into a small office, where the Chief Specialist came to speak with us. His words cut through the air like a knife when he solemnly stated, "Sophia has Retinoblastoma, a form of cancer that affects the eyes." His words seemed to ricochet around the room, leaving our hearts lodged firmly in our throats.

He explained, "The tumors originate in the retina, the light-sensitive eye layer responsible for vision. The pupil appears white instead of healthy black because the light hits the tumors. About 75% of cases involve only one eye, but Sophia's condition is bilateral stage 5B cancer. The 'B' classification indicates a seeding effect, like all the snow shaken in a snow globe."

All I could think was, "He cannot tell us that our baby has the worst stage of cancer in both of her eyes, and it is so advanced that the amount of cancer resembles the snow swirling in a shaken snow globe." The weight of his words, with the lack of compassion in his voice, hit me like a ton of bricks. He then told us that the only course of action was to remove both of her eyes. As we caught our breath, my husband and I informed him that we were people of faith and we would not agree to have Sophia's eyes removed unless God told us to.

He said, "Mrs. Roman, I am a man of science, and I believe this is the best chance at saving her life." The realization that I would witness my baby's suffering felt like an unavoidable reality crashing down upon us.

How can this happen to us? We have done everything by the book. We faithfully served God and

waited until after marriage to be intimate. Throughout the pregnancy, I adhered to strict dietary restrictions, limited caffeine intake, and avoided even a single aspirin for headaches. No one in our family has ever encountered this form of cancer before. I kept thinking, "This should not be happening to us!"

HOW MY FAITH BROUGHT ME THROUGH

I had not realized it then, but I harbored a sense of entitlement to a fairy-tale ending. We felt entitled to special treatment because of our dedication to serving God. We did not dare say that, of course, but that is what we felt in our hearts. With our daughter's sickness, our frustration and anger with God grew. I know now that being Christian does not shield us from trials. As Matthew 5:45 makes it clear, the rain falls on the righteous and the unrighteous, and we all share blessings and suffering. It is incredibly challenging to accept this reality, especially when we pray for others to receive their miracles but do not experience our own. This thinking causes many Christians to stumble. Too often, we mistakenly believe that surrendering our lives to God exempts us from hardship. However, whether one believes in Christ or not, life's storms are inevitable. The significant difference is that, as Christians, we have the power of the Holy Spirit within us, providing us with the strength to endure and the continual strengthening to emerge victorious from the storm.

The Plan

"And we know that all things work together for good for those who love God and are called according to his purpose." Romans 8:28 ESV

The next few weeks were a blur. We agreed not to decide to do anything until they gave Sophia an MRI. Our hearts overflowed with gratitude when the results revealed that the cancer had not extended beyond her eyes. Now, we were in a state of anticipation, seeking divine guidance on our next steps.

After presenting the results, the Chief Specialist mentioned that there might be an alternative to removing the eyes. He explained Sophia could be eligible for a new research procedure, given her age of six months and her stage 5B eye cancer. The Chief Specialist then informed us that he had arranged for Sophia to participate in a research study called Intra-arterial chemotherapy (IAC). He explained that a teaspoon-sized dose of chemotherapy would be administered into the ophthalmic artery, the primary blood supply at the back of the eye.

In laypeople's terms, they would insert a tube from her groin into the blood vessel of the eye to administer the chemo directly into it. This technique ensures significant amounts of chemotherapy target the eye while minimizing exposure to the rest of the body. Consequently, patients experience fewer side effects than conventional chemotherapy methods affecting the entire body. Due to the targeted area, fewer doses are needed than standard chemo protocols. Everything fell into place like a sign when I learned about this. Juan and I immediately felt this was the divine guidance we were praying for, and we felt overwhelming peace and gratitude for this option.

Now, it was beginning to dawn on us why the doctors had not detected the tumors during Sophia's early exams, or why my searches for "white in the eye" had turned up empty. It became clear that Sophia would not have been eligible for this new procedure if we had found out earlier. If Sophia were any younger than six months of age, the only option would be to remove both eyes.

As I looked back over the past few months, it was evident that every delay and setback was part of a more excellent plan orchestrated by God. He truly ordered our steps, and the delay was Romans 8:28 God's living Word working for Sophia's "good!"

With Sophia qualifying for this research procedure, our hopes soared, seeing it as the way God would provide the much-needed miracle to save her eyes. With survival rates as high as 95% for children with this type of cancer, Juan and I felt a surge of optimism for Sophia's future.

It seemed like our extended family took cues from our faith. There was no room for doubt; everyone rallied around the belief that Sophia would overcome this trial. We all held onto that belief while trusting in God to guide us through.

CHAPTER 3
Burden Lifter

"Come to me, all you who are weary and burdened, and I will give you rest." - Matthew 11:28 (NIV)

Gone were the days of worrying about tummy time and strolling to the library for Baby & Tots Storytime. It was like a bulldozer hit our world, leaving us to sift through the wreckage. While we were so grateful to God for the better option offered for our daughter, the shock of it all left us feeling numb. Processing the reality seemed as futile as trying to contain water with a colander.

The overwhelming sense of powerlessness was crushing. As parents, our innate instinct to shield our children from harm clashed with the monstrous presence of cancer. We found ourselves paralyzed, like spectators with limbs bound, unable to intervene and protect our baby from this invading force.

Amidst the chaos, the constant barrage of calls from worried loved ones only added to our overwhelming emotions. Every conversation made us relive our nightmare. I only wanted to hide beneath my covers and shut out the world. Then, like a light breaking in through the darkness, someone suggested the idea of starting a blog.

They directed me to CaringBridge, a global platform for sharing updates on one's health journey. It sounded like the lifeline I desperately needed—a way to ease the weight of constantly updating everyone without continuously revisiting the painful particulars. It became a burden-lifting tool to guide me through the tumultuous waters ahead.

After a few months of writing updates on Sophia's doctor's visits and test outcomes, the blog became more than a way to update loved ones. It evolved into a heartfelt expression, a lifeline through which I could process and voice my overwhelming emotions. Within the virtual confines of its pages, I found comfort in sharing the weight of our trials, inviting prayers and support from those who walked alongside us. Through moments of introspection, I unearthed profound reflections on the presence of God amidst the chaos—a reassurance that sustained me through the darkest days.

Each morning, as I faced the daunting reality of our circumstances, I felt an unyielding compulsion to make sense of this journey into which we were thrust. Clinging to the belief that every trial held a purpose, I found the strength to persevere—to extract lessons in resilience, compassion, and grit from the burden of adversity. Embracing this perspective became my lifeline—an anchor that fastened me to hope amidst the storm.

To my surprise, the blog exceeded my initial intentions. What had begun as a communication and personal therapy tool grew into a profound ministry tool spanning 157 pages. Publicly and privately, readers contacted me to share how my transparency profoundly impacted their lives. They found comfort in its words, prompting introspection and offering newfound insights into their lives.

One testimony stood out among the numerous heartfelt responses: a nurse shared how encountering Sophia and our family had reignited her faith in God. As we journey through the testimony, I am committed to weaving in blog entries that echo this sentiment. Within the testimony, the grey sections represent journal entries chronicling the period of our daughter's treatment. These entries offer an intimate glimpse into the emotional journey and challenges faced during this trying time.

CHAPTER 4
Treatment Phase 1

And Jesus asked him, "What do you want me to do for you?" And the blind man said to him, "Rabbi, let me recover my sight." And Jesus told him, "Go your way; your faith has made you well." And immediately, he recovered his sight and followed him on the way.
Mark 10:51-52 (ESV)

As we arrived at the hospital for Sophia's surgical procedure, a nurse named Bernice greeted us. Her demeanor radiated excitement as if she could not contain her joy at meeting us.

Without hesitation, she proclaimed, "This child is unique. Today, God will work a miracle through her. Just as He healed blind Bartimaeus, He will heal her."

Her words filled me with such happiness that I could not help but laugh joyfully, needing confirmation of the unexpected proclamation. I asked her to repeat it, wanting to soak in every word and reassure myself that I had heard correctly. She shared that she was on vacation and was not scheduled to work but called in at the last minute. She was certain God had brought her in to be present and see this miraculous baby.

In that divinely orchestrated moment, amidst the bustling uncertainty of the hospital corridors, Bernice's unwavering faith ignited a spark within us, flooding our hearts with the hope we yearned for—a hope for a miracle. It was evident that God had placed her there as a reminder of His constant presence, His boundless love for us, and the assurance that we are never alone. Reflecting on that encounter, I am amazed at how strategic God is. He used Bernice as a conduit to awaken a profound sense of expectation, knowing that is what cultivates the fertile ground for miracles, signs, and wonders to unfold. Oh, how I love Him!

Throughout the day, we felt immensely blessed. Every individual we encountered, from nurses to attendants to doctors, seemed like an angel sent to aid us. Their warmth, friendliness, and compassion enveloped us, which was a stark departure from the chilly atmosphere we faced during Sophia's first diagnosis at the cancer hospital among all those doctors.

Upon seeing our baby in recovery, the surreal feeling engulfed us. Sophia lay in the hospital crib, connected to various wires attached to her arms and toes, her leg confined in a splint, and my heart sank. Despite the ordeal, my resilient little warrior faced the day gracefully. As a parent, witnessing all that she had to endure was heart-wrenching, but amidst it all, I felt the strength of countless prayers lifting us and carrying us through the day. For that, I was deeply grateful.

A week and a half later, we returned to the specialist's office, eager to learn the outcome of Sophia's surgery.

January 27, 2009

Today marked Sophia's follow-up after her initial chemotherapy session. With local anesthesia administered, the medical team utilized ultrasound technology to assess the impact of the treatment on the tumors in her eyes. As we anxiously awaited, the specialist entered the room, his expression betraying a mix of surprise and relief. 'Is this the same child?' he exclaimed, visibly impressed. He proceeded to deliver the news we had been hoping for. All the tumors and seeds had been eradicated by the chemotherapy. I could not help but remark, 'Doc, we promised to make a believer out of you!'

His response was genuine amazement, and he remarked that Sophia's response to the treatment was the most remarkable they had seen to date. Praise God! He is faithful to His Word! God spoke of her healing, and it manifested before our eyes. (Sophia was diagnosed with the worst level of cancer; they first recommended the removal of the left eye and to treat the right eye. Then we were told she would need possibly four to six treatments of Chemo, and one treatment destroyed her cancer; this is unheard of!!!!)

Following the successful treatment, the Chief Specialist recommended a second surgery as a preventative measure to ensure the eradication of potentially undetected cells. With that completed, our focus shifted to follow-up care. We scheduled initial follow-up appointments to confirm the absence of cancer and monitor for any signs of recurrence.

After the second surgery, the Chief Specialist, who once proclaimed his disbelief in God but fully in science, now stood before us, urging us to pray for another miracle.

This time, it was for Sophia's retina to reattach. The detachment had occurred as the tumors grew. Surgery was not an option for retinoblastoma patients. Cutting the eye risked the chances of the cancer spreading. The test they performed to determine the electrical activity of the retina's reported less than 1% electrical response. That meant, according to the test, our baby was legally blind. According to the report, anyone around Sophia could testify that she sees. The question is, how well does she see?

So, we did what we knew best: we prayed and asked everyone who knew how to pray. It was another moment for God to demonstrate His power in Sophia's miracle, too.

NICOLE ESTELLE ROMAN

CHAPTER 5
It's Pouring

For I, the Lord your God, hold your right hand; I say,
"Fear not, I am the one who helps you."
Isaiah 41:13 (ESV)

When it rains, it pours! Just as we grappled with Sophia's diagnosis and prepared for her first surgery, another crisis struck. A few days after my father arrived from Florida for the holidays, he was rushed to the hospital. Suddenly, I found myself torn between two hospitals: one where my daughter was undergoing treatment and another where my father was fighting for his life.

All I could focus on was whether I could endure this perfect storm. My baby and my father, both in critical condition, weighed heavily on my heart. To truly grasp the depth of my anguish, one must understand that I am, unequivocally, a Daddy's girl. My father was not just my rock; he was the pillar I leaned on, my confidant, and my greatest fan.

I recall when my brother Steve, concerned about me being stretched from having to be there for Sophia and our dad at two different hospitals, suggested he could handle visiting Dad more on my behalf. While I appreciated his gesture to ease my burden, I could not entertain the thought of not being by my father's side. He had always been there for me, showering me with love and unwavering support. I could not bear the idea of him feeling abandoned by me in his darkest hour. So, despite the strain, I found myself going back and forth between two hospitals, determined to be there for both my baby and my dad.

During my visits to see my dad, he asked why my brother and I attempted to sneak him out of the hospital at night to take him to church. Reassuring him that no such plan happened, I could not help but smile, sensing that God was at work in his heart as he lay in the hospital bed. My constant prayer was that before my dad drew his last breath, he would accept Christ as his Savior. Therefore, I chose to believe that my dad's apparent confusion was not merely due to medication and his condition, but rather, he encountered God. That reassured me amidst the difficulty I was enduring, knowing that God, in His loving kindness, was drawing my father closer to Him.

Shortly after Sophia's second surgery, my father passed away. Deep within my heart, I am sure God orchestrated this timing. He had the opportunity to hear about the miraculous work of God, which I believe softened his heart in those final moments of life. While I was not present to witness it, I believe he surrendered his life to the Lord before drawing his last breath. Reflecting on this moment reminds me of the boundless love of my Heavenly Father.

My dad would not have been able to bear seeing Sophia or I suffer. His heart would have hardened towards God to the point of being unreachable. I believe God used the first miracle Sophia received to soften my dad's heart before he drew his last breath. I was there in those final moments of my dad's life.

As I heard the Holy Spirit tell me it was time, I whispered in my Daddy's ear that it was okay for him to go. I assured him I would be all right and loved him dearly. Placing my hand on his chest, I spoke softly, "I release your spirit back to God." Within seconds, the machine flatlined, and my dad peacefully passed away.

Death came knocking again, and now we have transitioned from a downpour to what felt like the perfect storm. Just as Sophia was recovering from her third surgery in May, mere days before Domonick's adoption was legally finalized, his biological brother fell victim to a senseless murder.

A chance encounter at a corner store with someone recently released from jail ended in a fatal stabbing. How could I possibly break this devastating news to my son? Sophia battling cancer, the recent loss of his grandfather, and now the murder of his biological brother.

With his brother's burial scheduled for a week later, we decided to delay telling Domonick about this heart-wrenching loss. We did not want it to cast a shadow over the joy of his official adoption into our family. He deserved a celebration, and with all we had been through so did we. After the court proceedings and the legal confirmation of his new name, Domonick Roman, we came together to celebrate as a family.

The next day we had to break the devastating news to our son about his brother's fate. So much sorrow packed into his short life and we were powerless to shield him from this as well. All we could do was cry out for strength to weather the relentless storms beating down on us.

HOW MY FAITH BROUGHT ME THROUGH

Life is not a fairytale; curveballs are inevitable, and sometimes, they strike back so forcefully that even the strongest individuals can be knocked down. Whether it is sickness, grief, abuse, or violence, these trials often come without warning. The only way to prepare is by strengthening your relationship with God. When you recognize He is your ever-present hope in times of trouble, you instinctively turn to Him when adversity strikes. In our moments of weakness, His strength sustains us, enabling us to weather life's most formidable storms.

Life will not always feel fair. Sometimes you may not understand why you must endure these fiery trials or face so many challenges. Through it all, I have learned that holding onto the injustice of it or having pity parties will not get you to the other side. I challenge you to hold onto God's unchanging hand and let His loving guidance lead you through the storm. When you face the worst life has to offer, turn to God and cling to Him until you see life "after _____" (Fill in the blank).

CHAPTER 6
Treatment-Advancing Forward

During the next monthly examination, the Chief Specialist discovered three tiny seeds in Sophia's left eye, each barely larger than a pencil point. This revelation came after she had undergone three rounds of surgical intra-arterial chemotherapy, during which numerous seeds and substantial tumors were eradicated.

The Chief Specialist remarked "now that the dust has settled, so to speak," they could now notice the cancer seeds on the film. Given their size, the doctor swiftly administered laser therapy while Sophia was under anesthesia in the office, a procedure that lasted about two minutes. The same treatment was done on Sophia's left eye a month later. We received encouraging test results.

May 12, 2009

The doctors were amazed that today Sophia has a 5% electrical response in her right eye. Back in March, the test reported less than 1% in both eyes. Currently, she has a 5% function of that eye. The doctor said, I know you are not amazed but we are because of the assault that was done to her eyes. I informed the Chief Specialist that he would be more amazed when God completely restore her vision.

He also said that it looks like the retina has attached in an area. Anyone who is around Sophia can testify that she sees more than the doctors' reports indicate. That is nothing but God. She is baffling the doctors every time we go...they do not know the God we serve! He is *shown just through her 11 months of life that He is a healer, deliverer, protector, restorer, faithful to his word, and a prayer answerer! Keep praying, I praise God that He is not done with her yet!"*

June 30, 2009

GOD IS STILL AMAZING ME!

Hallelujah, look who turned one! I must give God all the glory for the continuous healing He is doing in Sophia's eyes. For those who do not believe, your prayers get answered... Well, let me testify, they do! Sophia and I just left the cancer hospital for her six-week examination under anesthesia. The Chief Specialist came into the room I was waiting in with a release in his hands and a smile on his face. The examination detected a cancer seed in her left eye again. (Took less than 2 minutes to laser off) As he updated me on her progress, I asked the Chief Specialist if the function in Sophia's eye had increased, and he said no. He said not to get discouraged because it does not mean she cannot see; it is just a measure to help them determine what is happening.

I was a little sad, because I prayed God would increase the function in her eyes by the next visit. That was a lesson for me to ensure that I gather all the doctor reports and seek the report of the Lord. Then, the doctor who performed the function test came into the room with a report in his hands and was smiling. He said, "Doctor, there has been a minor improvement in Sophia's right eye. The function has increased by one and ½ percent, which has doubled since the last visit. Then the Chief Specialist looked at me and said, "I stand corrected, she has had improvement in her eye function." Right there, my mouth dropped open.

Then I asked what was going on with her retina. Have they attached a little more since the last visit? The doctor informed me that her retinas in both eyes have completely attached! I was amazed. I had to ask again to ensure I was clear in what he said. For those of you who do not know this, the doctors could not surgically attach them for fear of cancer spreading throughout her body. The doctor told us several months ago that we would have to ask God for "another miracle to be performed on her," which was to reattach her retinas.

Well, let me testify that God answered those prayers! The Chief Specialist said a visiting doctor from California was in the examination room. After comparing Sophia's film to her initial examination, the results blew him away. He said I cannot believe this is the same child. The Chief Specialist said this is nothing short of miraculous! He told me to keep praying because it seemed to work! Wow! God is showing the doctors where they end and where He begins!

August 18, 2009

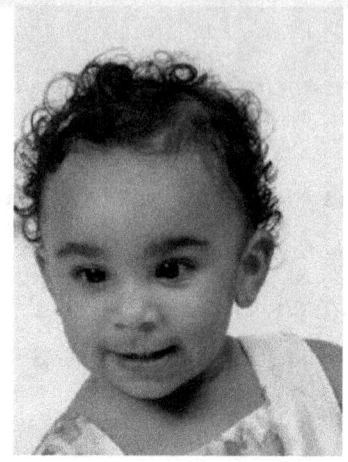

AGAINST THE ODDS

"Stand still and see the salvation" is the scripture that comes to mind when I think about everything Sophia had to overcome these past eight months. From her initial diagnosis to where we are today, Sophia is truly a testament to God's healing powers." Not so," said God when the specialist recommended eye removal. God said not so when the doctors said it would take the maximum number of surgeries to administer the chemo, (six), but He destroyed, the cancer in one. When the doctor said she had a massive assault against her eyes (he used those words...not knowing he was in the spirit), God destroyed the tumors that were too many to count before the doctors' eyes. God said not so when the doctors said her retinas

may never reattach. God has set it up so that no one can take the credit for Sophia's healing but God!

God blew on every hurdle before her, and the situation turned in her favor. Not because of anything we did or did not do. Not because Sophia is more unique than the other children who did not have such a favorable outcome. That was God's plan for healing this child because He knew in His infinite wisdom that each person attached to this trial needed to know that God was real and that He was still in the miracle business. I am so thankful that my father got to see that for himself before his passing.

God received His glory when each of us shared this testimony beyond those who know her. I cannot even count how many strangers were brought to tears hearing about what God had done. Or how many reports from friends and family who have shared Sophia's story, and those who heard how God moved. Sophia not even knowing it has been used by God to show people that God still answers prayers. That the miracles that are in the Bible are not far reaching but God is still in the miracle business.

This past Tuesday, Sophia had her six-week examination under anesthesia. The great news is that there is still no reoccurrence of cancer!!!! The same three cancer seeds she had lasered three times already were lasered again. When the doctor briefed me on Sophia's status, I asked why her eye moved inwards and how long it would take for the muscle to heal. The Chief Specialist informed me that eyes damaged by cancer move inward, looking for a place to see through the retinas.

So basically, as the tumors grew out of the retinas, the place where they grew has destroyed that part of the retinas. So, in Sophia's case, more than half of her left retina is killed by cancer and a little less than half of the right eye. The doctor said the destroyed parts of the retina do not regenerate itself. He said it was like a stroke. When destroying those parts of the brain, the other parts try to compensate for the damaged parts. He said it would take months to know how much she can see. I do not know how God will show up in this, but I know God is against the odds. He has repeatedly proven Sophia's healing. For those who believe in the power of prayer, I humbly request your prayers for Sophia's complete restoration of her retinas. May her retinas function at their optimum level, resulting in full vision restoration. While the doctors have provided their prognosis, let us remember that ultimately, it is in God's hands, and He has the final say!

HOW MY FAITH BROUGHT ME THROUGH

September 24, 2009

HOW A MOTHER SEE'S IT...

Sophia had her six-week eye examination under anesthesia on Tuesday. That sounds so simple because the words do not accurately paint the picture. Going through this for over ten months has become a routine. But today, I thought about it. When so much stuff happens, you operate on autopilot.

The night before we take her to the hospital, we have to keep her up as long as possible. This way, she is exhausted in the morning and does not think about having a bottle. (Prayerfully) We then wake her up around midnight and try to keep her up until 1 am so she can have her last bottle. Sophia cannot have any milk or food for at least six hours before her appointment because she has to have anesthesia.

Then we had to get up at 5 am to get dressed in the dark so Sophia would not wake up when we left the house at 5:30 am. Then, what we dread happens: Sophia wakes up as we transport her to the car. She cries for a bottle, but I cannot give her one, and I hope and pray she falls back asleep.

Sophia and I got to the hospital for her 6:30 am appointment. In the waiting room, I look around to see how many children look younger than Sophia. See, the youngest goes first. If there are many children, it will take longer to prevent the baby from wanting a bottle.

There are children of all ages and nationalities from different parts of the country, with other stories and treatments. Some of them have lost their eyes. Some only had cancer in one. Some were having chemo treatments in their state, and parents heard about the great results the NY Cancer Hospital was having with the research procedure. So, some kids come in with the effects of regular chemo, hair loss, and pale skin. When you sit there and really think about it, and allow yourself to feel, it is *overwhelming. You must then shake it off so you can be strong for your child.*

Then, one couple always looks scared to death, sitting in the waiting room. They are the first timers. They are the ones who found out from another doctor that their child may have cancer, and they need to go to the NY Cancer Hospital for more tests. My heart goes out to them because I remember being in their shoes. Scared to death that what you dread will be told to you. Then they take the parents in the back. The child gets examined. About a half hour later, they return to the waiting room, holding their baby and each other while crying.

I sit there trying to shake off the tears because it is like I relive the pain of first hearing about Sophia again. I usually see this play out every time I come because these babies are always younger than Sophia, so they go first. The nurse comes, and the struggle begins... Sophia's eyes need to be dilated for them to examine her.

So, I have to take her into the back, put her down on a stretcher, and hold her little hands. One nurse holds her head, and another pries her eyelids open to put the drops in while Sophia is screaming the entire time. Every time I bring her back, she clings to my shirt with all her strength while I say, "Baby, this is to help you." I feel like when she clings to me, she is trying to say, "Mommy, why are you letting them do this to me?" This process usually happens three times before her eyes are ready.

Then, after two hours of her being awake and trying to keep her mind off milk, they finally called me back into the examination room. The doctors filled the room about fifteen deep. Most of them are resident or visiting doctors from around the country. As you walk past their seemingly sympathetic looks, you feel all their eyes on you. I almost had to pretend they were not in the room to keep moving. I then laid Sophia down on the examination table. Once again, I held her arms while a nurse tried to hold her head in place for the anesthesiologist to put the mask on her face. After she fights for about two minutes, her body finally surrenders to the drugs.

I then go into a waiting room and wait until the doctor tells me if there is any reoccurrence of cancer. Praise God that I only received good news. The three cancer dots on her left eye were finally dead. That was the first time since the chemo that Sophia did not have to have a laser on her left eye. Then they bring Sophia out about half an hour later, groggy and screaming. She screams because she wakes up scared. After all, Sophia does not know what will happen next and cries for her bottle and

Mommy. I then must calm her down and reassure her that I am here. Then we drove home. She has been out of it for hours.

When she wakes up, I must wipe the glue between her lashes. She wakes up screaming through the night most of the time after she goes for her examination. On examination days, we do not even try to put her in her crib. She sleeps between us. Sometimes, with one arm on Daddy and the other hand on Mommy. Sometimes, we take turns holding her. I do not know whether it is more to comfort her or us. Then, six weeks later, we had to go through it again.

November 10, 2009

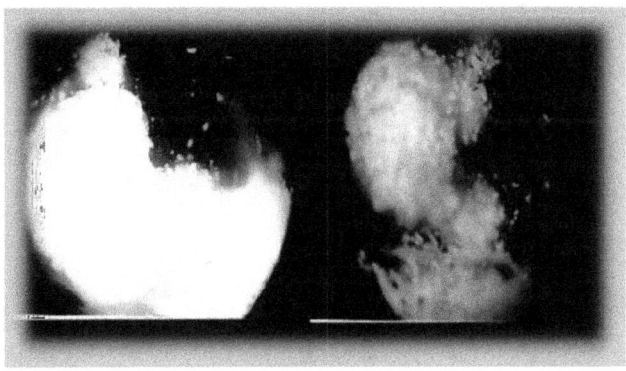

IT IS A PART OF THE PROCESS

This morning, I had to take Sophia to the cancer hospital for her six-week eye examination. As they say, a *mother always knows. I dreaded bringing her because I knew in my spirit that I would not get a favorable report today. Why? I do not know, maybe because in the past few weeks, I have told so many people about her miraculous healing, and I felt an attack coming. Or perhaps I'm beginning to understand that there is always a process behind an incredible testimony.*

As I mature, I accept that things will not always be easy, and a true victory comes with a price. The price is the process you must go through for a testimony. Through the process, you learn where you end, and God begins. It is through the process that we are to draw closer to God. It is through this process that we better understand His importance and power. Through the process, we develop spiritual muscles to weather more significant storms.

I felt the heaviness of the price this morning as I dressed in the dark. As Juan carried Sophia to the car, I got into the driver's seat and wanted to throw a tantrum. I did not want to deal with the process. Nor did I want to go through the process by myself today. I felt like kicking and screaming and asking Juan to take off work to come with me. He would have come if I had asked, but I did not because it is part of my process.

HOW MY FAITH BROUGHT ME THROUGH

I got to the hospital in record time. Sophia was the first patient to get there at 6:20 am. Within five minutes, we held her down to put the eye drops in her eyes as she fought. After an hour, her eyes were dilated and ready to be examined. As I laid her on the examination bed and they started administering the anesthesia, I thought about how tired I was watching her go through this process. As I waited for her to recover, the Chief Specialist came into the consulting room to update me on her situation.

As soon as I saw him, I took a deep breath and thought, "Here we go." He said everything looked good. I looked at him and said, "There's a catch." And he said, "Yes, there is. I guess me coming in with a chart indicated that." He told me that a new tumor had formed on the edge of Sophia's retina in her left eye. The tumor was the size of a pencil point, and the laser would not reach it. As he put the consent form in front of me, he informed me that they would do cryotherapy, which is freezing the tumor. The doctor places a probe (which looks like a pen) on the sclera nearest the tumor, using a freezing gas to freeze and thaw the cancer several times. That destroys the tumor cells and leaves a flat, pigmented scar with no signs of tumor. If the cancer is evident, the doctor repeats the treatment until all the tumor cells are destroyed.

He informed me that due to Sophia's eyelid swelling, I had to apply ointment twice daily for a few days. He then told me that cancer is common in small children with this condition. He said as the retina grows, the chance for reoccurrence is great. Once patients become adults, the reoccurrence usually stops because no more growth exists in the eye. As he left the room, I tried hard to keep the tears from rising. I was not fearful, nor was my faith wavering. I am still standing steadfast by His word. But you see, the mother in me grieved for my baby. Something I cannot shield her from or take away. All I can do is love her through the process.

So, I made the next appointment for December 15th. We will pray, believe, and hope for the best, but knowing what comes our way is part of the process. So, we left, and I drove home with the baby sleeping as tears poured as I tried to release the weight of the process. I am so thankful that some doctors are skilled in finding early detection and technology to treat it. This minor setback does not take away from the fantastic victory she has already experienced. The picture above puts everything in perspective.

The first white mass is the live cancer, and the second is the destroyed cancer. Her eyes survived the

HOW MY FAITH BROUGHT ME THROUGH

massive assault of cancer. She did not lose sight nor her life. God is so good! I may be tired of the process, but I am so thankful God has shown up in this process!

During the monthly check-ups, Sophia's eye required treatment for the same three seeds. The doctor lasered two; the third demanded cryotherapy to address its stubbornness. Looking back, I wish I had the knowledge I have now. I could not advocate effectively for my daughter because I lacked awareness of what to look for. Shockingly, Sophia had not undergone an MRI since December 2008. This oversight is a stark reminder that, as caregivers, we may not always know which questions to ask when faced with adversity. While we trust specialists to guide us, we must acknowledge that doctors, subject to human limitations, practice medicine and can make mistakes. We must become proactive advocates for our loved ones and ourselves, questioning, comprehending procedures, and insisting on clear follow-up plans. Our vigilance can mean the difference between life and death.

I am amazed that during Sophia's two and a half years of treatment, neither pediatricians nor specialists requested another MRI despite knowing the risk of cancer spreading. Given Sophia's persistent active seeds and the severity of her cancer, regular MRI check-ups every six months should have been standard. If your gut feeling tells you something is wrong, DO NOT ignore it. If doctors hesitate to run a test, insist on it in writing.

Seek second opinions, ask about warning signs, and educate yourself on the topic. Demand clear explanations from healthcare professionals, even if they seem reluctant to provide them.

Let Sophia's story serve as a cautionary tale and a call to action for all parents and caregivers to relentlessly seek information and guidance to give their children the best care. Ask God to guide you to your needed revelation and be vigilant in advocating for the health and well-being of your loved ones. Trust your instincts and actively pursue the answers and care your family needs. Since the November 10, 2009, journal entry, Sophia has been visiting the hospital for eye check-ups every six weeks, undergoing treatments for the three cancer seeds in her left eye. This routine persisted until her second birthday in June 2010. The journal picks up again in August 2010, documenting the progression of the disease.

August 5, 2010

FAITH TESTED

As Sophia was under anesthesia, the doctor came into the room, and I immediately knew there was a next step to take when I saw forms in his hands. For a year, whenever examined, three spots in her left eye needed additional treatment, and I have to give my consent. Time stands still for a moment, with the anticipation of losing my breath. It is not that I do not believe in her healing or God is in control. However, one thing I have learned about faith is that a process comes with it.

From the time God gives a Word to the moment it manifests, the time between is the process, or what some people call the wait. That is the testing of your faith. It is what you must go through to get to the manifestation. This time, it shows YOU what you are made of. It shows how much you trust God and allows you to draw closer to the King of Kings. It is when you know your limitations without God and the endless possibilities with Him working through you.

God never told Juan and me that Sophia was coming out of this quickly. God said He would heal her; this was our trial to build our faith. He told me not to write a script of how He would do it. So here I am, waiting to see how God will flex again.

The doctor informs me that the three dots in Sophia's left eye have gotten a little bigger. We have been treating that area for over a year with laser, and it is time to explore another option. I heard his words as he was talking, but they were not registering. The wind knocked out of me. I told him I had to call my husband and put him on speaker because I knew I needed another set of ears for this.

The doctor recommended using radioactive plaques. Radioactive plaques are custom-built for each child. Sophia would have to be hospitalized and undergo two separate operations (one to insert the plaque and one to remove it). The reason the doctor recommended the plaques is because they reach the surface of the tumor. The long-term effects, possibly including cataracts, radiation retinopathy, and impaired vision, may occur. Due to its radioactive nature, pregnant women, and children under twelve are advised not to come near her while she is in the hospital.

If we agree to do this, setting up will take ten days. So, Juan and I decided to have her left eye lasered during that visit, and we would return in three weeks to re-examine her again. We told him we would pray whether we would move forward with the surgery or not. If God says to go forward, we will, but I have not heard the Lord speak on this yet.

So, I will make my petition now! So please, touch and agree with us that within the next three weeks God moves in her favor. That God gives us a miracle encore! He shows up so mightily that the doctor returns and says I need to know the God you serve! That God not only shrinks the spots but also the cancer cells. Such a mighty healing occurs in Sophia's left eye; the retina completely reattaches, and the vision is restored. The film does not have a trace of a tumor, dead or living! GOD IS ABLE!

August 25, 2010

I will not die, but live and proclaim what the LORD has done. Psalm 118:17 (NIV)

Three weeks flew by and I brought Sophia to her follow-up eye exam this past Tuesday. Our last report was that the doctor recommended surgery. I was a little unnerved about attaching a radioactive plaque to her eye.

Sophia, Dom, and I walked into the office that morning, and only two children were waiting for the doctor to see them. I breathed a sigh of relief because this meant we would be out of there faster and Sophia would not have to wait long to eat or drink. The children had to go under anesthesia (that is why they could not have anything in their stomachs) to do the procedure, and they put clamps on their eyes to keep the lids open.

As we waited our turn, the waiting room filled with other patients and their families. Almost 95% of the children examined that day had an eye removed. Because they were so small, they did not have prosthetic eyes, and their parents did not opt to cover the eye socket. That was unusual to see. Usually, one or two kids have had an eye removed and always wear their prosthetic eye. Keeping it real, my heart got heavier as I watched each child. The Devil was playing with my fears. I was trying to shake off negative thoughts that were trying to infiltrate my mind. Is God trying to tell me this is Sophia's fate? Is He preparing me for this step?" I had to keep talking to myself.

I was trying to combat every negative thought with a positive one. Thinking, "God brought her this far, He won't leave her now." Or "how would this bring God's glory after He performed a miracle to save her eye to lose it now?" I brought Sophia to the exam room. I put her on the table, screaming, and crying. The nurse held her head as I held her hands. They put the mask on her over her nose/mouth and started administering the anesthesia.

I began talking to her about Barney, Riff, BJ, and Baby Bop. I was thinking to myself, this is her cross to bear. No matter what I say or do, I cannot shield her. I CAN'T CONTROL the one thing I wish I could! I HAVE TO TRUST that God is in control, and He is watching over her while I leave my baby on a hospital bed in a room of doctors and machines. I went into the consultation room as the doctors conducted Sophia's examination.

Domonick enters the room and says, "Mom, I was so scared and wanted to cry, but I didn't want to do it in front of the children." I said why? He said, "because all the kids who had their eye removed." He said, "I have a better understanding of Phia's testimony... of what God did for her." I said, "Today, made it real for you." He said, "Yes." At that moment, I let a few tears drop. The Chief Specialist came in about 10 minutes later to tell me that the left eye had shown a definite response to the laser from the last visit. The tumors treated decreased in size. We conferenced Juan in by phone and decided to laser the two tumors and cyro the third (freeze the hard-to-reach area).

After I signed the release, the doctor handed me and Domonick a book a 7-year-old wrote about her experience with this disease. As the doctor closed the door, all the tears I tried to hold back came down like a tidal wave.

Reading that little girl's book made me cry more. I was crying because of the goodness of the Lord. I was crying because of the favor God had shown my family. I was crying because even in the victory, this was a trial that my entire family was going through. I was crying for all the children who lost an eye and for their parents. I was crying for the caregivers, those who go to work every day and experience the highs and lows of cancer.

When Sophia came out of the examination room her left eye was swollen. As we got into the car, she kept crying and screaming, "my eye." Because of the freezing of the tumor (it is like a burn on the eye), she could not open her eyes. So, I drove with my left hand and reached back to hold her hand with my right while tears kept falling. She kept screaming; all I could do was call on the one in control. I started to pray that God soothed her eye, give her peace and that sleep overtakes her. Before I said AMEN, she was sleeping. Domonick said, "That was awesome, how God responded that quickly." Tears fell with joy! A few hours later, she was playing. The ordeal wiped me out. Kids are resilient!

The next day, my sister-friend Jenice called me to talk about a dream she had involving Sophia. In the dream, we were in a hotel room when suddenly Sophia started shaking and rolling her eyes back. I held her hand while this was happening. In the dream, Jenice explained Sophia was having a seizure. After it ended, Sophia went back to playing.

After I hung up the phone, I knew the dream was a warning from God. Jenice often has prophetic dreams, and I believed God was preparing me for something about to happen in His loving mercy. To my surprise, within just six days, I experienced the exact situation she had dreamed about.

CHAPTER 7
Treatment Escalates

September 1, 2010

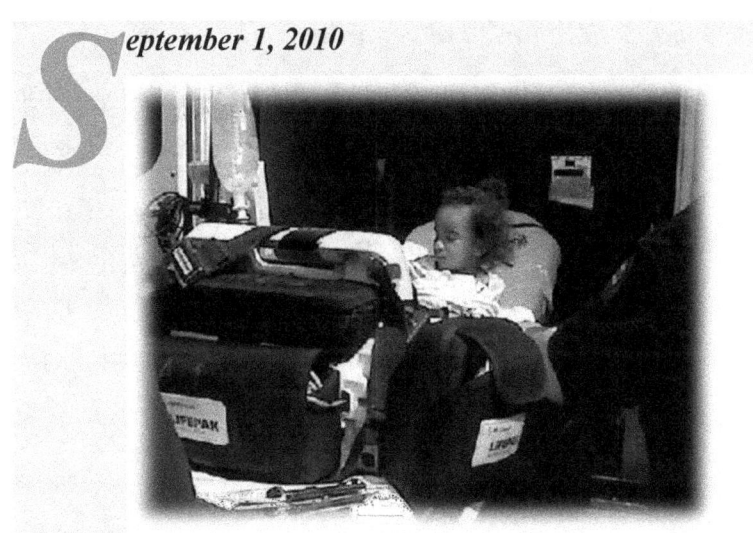

Beloved, think it not strange concerning the fiery trial, which is to try you, as though some strange thing happened unto you: But rejoice, since ye are partakers of Christ's sufferings; that, when his glory shall be revealed, ye may be glad also with exceeding joy. 1 Peter 4:12-13 (KJV)

Sophia woke up around 5:40 am crying. At first, I did not think anything of it because it was not out of the ordinary. Then, around 6 am, she started throwing up the milk she had previously drank. From 6 am to 8 am, she kept throwing up. We assumed it was stomach flu because a baby boy from our church was throwing up over the weekend. Around 8 am, Sophia seemed listless. She was spitting up while trying to keep it back.

Then one of her eyes and cheek were twitching, while simultaneously, her mouth was moving in a closed chewing motion. I tried to get dressed while putting her on her side, calling Juan on one phone and her pediatrician on the other. I knew something was wrong but did not know what to do. I got her dressed and raced to the car. As I got her into the car, Juan pulled up. Thank God he has had experience with someone with seizures. The seizures went on for about an hour. After that, Sophia was nonresponsive until about noon.

The CAT scan showed what the doctor thought was a small amount of blood on the right side of her brain, probably responsible for the seizures. Then they told us there was a mass in her brain. They had to transfer her to a hospital in NY to see a neurologist. Sophia and I got in the ambulance and headed to New York, while Juan and Dom followed in the car.

So many doctors, doctors in training, fellows, nurses, RNs, and Child Life Team came in and out. I had to repeat the morning events until the point of exhaustion. The assistant neurologist informed us that the mass was sitting in the back of the brain, hindering the flow of fluid to the brain. That likely was the cause of the nausea and throwing up. Each doctor had speculated what was going on from the CAT scan but would no longer commit to anything until she received an MRI.

They scheduled the MRI for the following day. Today felt like a sucker punch. It's almost like this cannot be real. It felt like I was having a bad dream that I could not wake up from. Fear tried to paralyze me from acting this morning. As I watched my daughter lying in her hospital bed, all I could think was, "Jesus help us," and praying that there was one more miracle left for our household.

September 2, 2010

But they that wait upon the LORD shall renew their strength; they shall mount with wings as eagles; they shall run, not be weary; they shall walk, and not faint. Isaiah 40:31 (KJV)

Sophia had an MRI of her brain and spine. The MRI revealed a tumor in the back of her brain and a layer of coating of tumor cells on the right/left side of the brain and in the spine. The nurses immediately prepared Sophia for surgery. The neurosurgeon tried to bypass the pressure, but there was a thin layer of tumor cells covering the tumor, which made it dangerous to puncture. So, he took a biopsy of the cancer and removed some fluid in the brain.

The good news is that the tumor does not cover the flow completely; about 25% of the flow was still not blocked. The doctors removed fluid from Sophia's spine through a tube from her head attached to a machine to temporarily drain the excess fluid in her brain. Sophia then had a second procedure. The doctor placed an implantable port into her chest. It is a thin, soft plastic tube put into a vein in her chest and has an opening (port) just under the skin. That allows medicines to go into the vein. They did this because the doctors anticipated Sophia would start chemo, and this would be easier than consistently putting IVs into her.

HOW MY FAITH BROUGHT ME THROUGH

September 3, 2010

Fear thou not; for I am with thee be not dismayed; for I am thy God: I will strengthen thee; yea, I will help thee; yea, I will uphold thee with the right hand of my righteousness.
Isaiah 41:10 (KJV)

Later in the day, Sophia had a shunt surgically implanted. Shunting is surgery to relieve increased pressure inside the skull due to excess fluid in the brain. It is internal piping. The surgeon put a small hole into the brain and made a surgical cut behind the ear and another small surgical cut in the belly. A small, thin tube called a catheter passes into a ventricle of the brain. Another catheter is placed under the skin behind the ear and moved down the neck, chest, and abdomen. Unfortunately, a valve (fluid pump) was placed under the skin by her hairline. The programmable valve is attached to both catheters. When extra pressure builds around the brain, the valve opens, and excess fluid drains into the belly or chest area. That helps decrease intracranial pressure.

While we were in the waiting room, my mind was racing. I felt fear trying to take hold of me. My imagination was moving at warp speed. I was writing scripts while dreams flashed before my eyes, and I started to hyperventilate. The walls were closing in, and I felt faint.

The nightmare continued, and I could not press pause, stop, or eject. It had to play out whether I wanted it to or not.

The bone of my bone and flesh of my flesh, my baby, the only child I pushed out from my body, was on an operating table, and I felt utterly helpless. Not that I do not trust God. I know enough that trust does not necessarily mean you will receive your desired outcome. At this point, I could not even say, "Jesus help us" "All I could get out was "Jesus" repeatedly.

I know Juan had his moments of release when I was not looking, probably when he walked back from the operating room or when he slipped away for a few moments. That is the burden of being a Priest. You must be strong for everyone. My heart went out to him. I was grateful Dom was with a friend. It would have been too much for him.

Sophia came out of surgery and I was able to get myself together. I watched her as she slept. I was thanking God for the warm blood flowing in her body. Then, I had to go home and tell my son about the fight we had ahead of us. That night, I set up a mattress on the floor for Dom in my room, knowing he needed to feel as close to me as I did to him.

September 7, 2010

Today, I had to bring Sophia in for some tests to see if the cancer had spread to other places in the body. The first test was a stomach scan. The test showed there was no cancer in the liver. Sophia also had a bone marrow fluid and marrow extraction done. (A few days later, the test came back negative). Thank You, Jesus!

September 8, 2010

"They overcame him by the blood of the Lamb and by the word of their testimony..." Rev 12:11(NIV)

Today, Phia had a bone scan done to rule out cancer in her bones. Thank God the test came back negative. As Juan and I were waiting for Phia's test, a woman overheard the frustration I was having from a doctor about the hospital retrieving my daughter's biopsy slides from another hospital. She approached me and handed me a CD called "A Warfare Prayer." She said she knew she would give it to someone today and knew in her spirit that it was for me.

She went on to minister to me about not letting the devil get me in an uproar over stupid stuff and to keep fighting and believing until God says otherwise. She also told my husband and me we needed to get something out of this trial. (Which is confirmation). She was what I needed at the right time: an answered prayer. I asked God to send someone without connection to us to give me a word and He did. He is awesome.

After the test, I met with the Pediatric Doctor to discuss the treatment plan that the team recommends. Phia has what they call "Extra-ocular retinoblastoma or trilateral retinoblastoma." The treatment is extensive chemotherapy administered over 6-8 months. He was optimistic about the success rate. This condition was previously fatal. They said 30 to 40 percent of patients now live a cancer-free life. He felt hopeful about Sophia's chances. He went on to say that this type of cancer responds well to chemo. After we met and he briefed me on the pros and cons, we went home and tried to rest. I told the doctor I would get back to him when we were ready. That night, Juan and I prayed, and we both heard God say to start on Wednesday. So, we had a week to pull ourselves together, enjoy our daughter, and pretend everything was normal.

HOW MY FAITH BROUGHT ME THROUGH

September 14, 2010

Ye are of God, little children, and have overcome them: because greater is he in you than in the world.
1 John 4:4 (KJV)

Yesterday and today, Sophia did not want to do anything but lie down. She would not eat (for those who know her, that is cause for alarm). Whenever you tried to move her, she would say, "I want to sleep." She got up when I was not in the room to find me, and she was wobbling and holding onto things. She was walking like she was trying to walk for the first time. I called the hospital and spoke to the team, and they said to keep monitoring her but they did not seem too concerned. Later that day, I emailed the Oncology Pediatric Doctor, expressing my concerns about starting chemo when she was already in pain and weak. That night, she was in so much pain. Sophia was crying and screaming all night. I gave her some pain medicine, but it brought little comfort.

~~~~~

Looking back on this journal entry, I regret not pushing for further examinations. I had a strong feeling that something was off. I have learned that cancer signs can show up in various ways for different people. Sometimes, what doctors might not see as a red flag can be crucial. My daughter's body was giving us signals that something was not right, but the doctors suggested keeping an eye on her. As advocates, we must stand firm and insist on further action when we know something is going on that causes our alarm bells to go off.

September 15, 2010

In his kindness, God called you to share in his eternal glory through Christ Jesus. So, after you have suffered a little while, he will restore, support, and strengthen you and place you on a firm foundation.
1 Peter 5:10 (NIV)

We brought Sophia into the hospital to start the Chemo treatment. Before starting, I voiced my concerns about Sophia's health. I insisted on a test on her head. Juan and I thought maybe the shunt was not working correctly, causing significant pain. She received a CAT scan and then we were brought to the outpatient bed area. This area is where children receive their chemo. It is like an emergency hospital waiting area with many cubes, like rooms with a bed and a TV for the children to be comfortable for the day-long process. As I am sitting there trying to keep Sophia calm while we wait for the results of the CAT scan, I am trying to fight back the tears.

HOW MY FAITH BROUGHT ME THROUGH

I hear children's cries, screams, and moans bellowing through the air, encircling me like stale cigarette smoke that does not move on a hot summer day. I felt overwhelmed but tried to hold it together for Phia's sake. My mind wondered when we first walked into the clinic today and saw a teenage girl throwing up blood in the waiting area. Juan and I tried to block it out, but how could we? We did not speak about it, as I am sure our minds thought about Phia's future struggles.

Then my thoughts went back to a year and a half ago when I was so thankful not to have to bring Sophia to the ninth floor of the cancer hospital. The ninth-floor houses children with all kinds of cancers for treatment. The place is decorated beautifully for children. It is bright and colorful. It has computer stations, a game room, chairs, and small sofas. There is even a pantry where you can get free juice and coffee. But outside the pleasantries, you see children of all ages with different levels of sickness.

If you allow yourself to take it all in, you truly see children who have lost their hair or body parts, have sores, or are in a wheelchair or on crutches. You see kids weak and lying on the small sofas or the little ones playing in the play area. You see children and their families with their lives on hold. You see the desire for a miracle in their eyes, with the reality of the disease on their face.

Unfortunately, now we are these families, and this is our child's struggle for life. The doctors felt it was OK to proceed with the chemo. After 6 pm, the nurses moved Phia to the inpatient area. We shared a room with a 3-year-old girl named Rachel, who was diagnosed with an incurable cancer that attacks the nervous system. Rachel was in so much pain she cried through the night, which made Sophia cry all night, too. I am sure Rachel's mom shed tears like I did. As I tried to comfort my daughter while praying for both children, I tried to find a place to go in my mind where I could let numbness wash over me.

September 16, 2010

These things I have spoken unto you, that in me ye might have peace. In the world ye shall have tribulation: but be of good cheer; I have overcome the world.
John 16:33 (KJV)

Today was day two of Sophia's Chemo. Phia was uncomfortable; she would cry whenever you tried to move her. I knew this was not because of the chemo and I kept telling the doctors that. She was not moving around much, not even kicking her legs. There was still some movement in *her feet, though. The doctors kept saying, "We will keep watch of this." She started throwing up today from the drugs. I was moving on autopilot, cleaning up the mess one after another. Juan came to relieve me. I knew I had to get some rest, because I needed my strength for the fight ahead.*

September 17, 2010

Hold unswervingly to the hope we profess, for He who promised is faithful.
Hebrews 10:23 (NIV)

When I got to the hospital, Juan informed me that Phia had not been moving her feet or legs. When he mentioned it to the nurses, they said they would notify the doctors. When I inquired, the answer was the same. I then called the head neurologist on duty. A little later, a team of neurologists came in.

The neurologist said Phia was temporarily paralyzed. She told me the chemo could cause it to attack the bad cells, causing swelling. They were trying to move quickly to get her an MRI. Quickly, was hours later. After the MRI, they moved us back into the Pediatric Observation Unit, because now her case was more serious. A doctor from the neurosurgeon team came in to reprogram the pressure on Sophia's shunt.

I asked him about the results of the MRI. He told me the MRI showed that the tumor layer on Sophia's spine became thicker (worse), which was putting more compression on the spine. That was blocking the fluid flow from moving around the spine. That caused the fluid to hit directly into the spine. That is what was causing Sophia the pain, which started a week ago when she did not want to get up, play, eat, and began to walk funnily.

The neurosurgeon said they would not recommend surgery at this time, because it would be too extensive. He was hopeful, though; he said Sophia had a good chance because of her age. I felt sick to my stomach and faint. I was trying to stay calm, but on the inside, I was screaming please, God let this cup pass.

September 18, 2010

"For my thoughts are not your thoughts, neither are your ways my ways," declares the LORD.
Isaiah 55:8 (NIV)

Today, Sophia had three MRIs taken, two on the head and one on her neck. The neurologist team came in at 2:15 pm to view the images from today and from September

2. They took a long time, so I knew it could not be good. I requested the imaging, so they sent it to me when ready. As they went through the images, I felt like the blood was draining from my veins. I felt all their eyes on me while watching each image.

The head neurologist talked, and I felt like her words bounced off me. It was almost unbelievable how much the cancer progressed in the brain and spine. It looked like the cancer was trying to devour the brain. The layer of the tumor covered the length of the spine. It caused the fluid of the spine to be blocked and hit into the spine. That was causing pain and temporary paralysis.

The image of September 2 was horrible but felt manageable. But the photos from this recent MRI were unbelievable. I knew that no matter how much chemo they gave her, medicine was not going to heal her. Only the healing hand from God can turn this situation around and ensure victory. As I looked at the images, I had a flashback to the pictures of my father's brain after he suffered a massive stroke. I felt weak to my knees. I prayed silently that when I got up from the chair, God would strengthen me and that I would not collapse in front of the team of doctors.

The Nurse Practitioner came into the room and asked me if I ever cry (OK, those who know me...my nickname from my brothers was crybaby). I said yes, of course. I tried to explain to her that I cannot afford to break down whenever I get bad news. I heard the doctor's report, but I am seeking God, for that is the only report that matters. I went on to tell her that I must believe and hold onto that the Word of God, that all of this must be working for my good.

God is genuinely pulling ministry out of us and pouring something into us. I told her that when I am weak, God is strong. Right now, I am only standing because God answered the prayers of the righteous for my strength. That is a day-by-day and moment-by-moment situation.

September 21, 2010

Whenever a doctor or nurse comes near Phia, she says, "Be nice." It is Phia's saying not to hurt or leave me alone. It has become a source of amusement for the staff at the hospital.

Phia worked with physical and musical therapy today. While they sang and played games, Phia kept telling them to be nice. The musical therapist then made up a "be nice" song. It was one of the highlights of the day.

HOW MY FAITH BROUGHT ME THROUGH

> *Phia gave the therapists a hard time, but it was due to the heavy dose of steroids she was taking. The mood swings are out of this world. When the neurologist examined her, she began to move her toes. Praise God!*

~~~~

Reflecting on the following six entries in the journey, I cannot help but think about all the challenges that come with cancer or any illness. It is as though each issue triggers a domino effect, setting off a chain reaction where one problem inevitably leads to another. From the initial diagnosis of cancer in Phia's eyes to its spread to her brain and spine, each step seemed to bring a new complication. Loss of feeling in her legs, drop foot, bladder infections, mood swings from steroids, and the need for a blood transfusion.

Years later, these experiences continue to serve as vivid reminders of the complexities of illness. It is crucial to see beyond the surface of illness to deepen our empathy and understanding for others facing health challenges. Remember, there is often more to someone's health journey than meets the eye. As you read the journal entries, take a moment to reflect and pray for those who are sick, in the hospital, facing illness, and for the people supporting them.

Gracious and Merciful God,

We lift to you all those who are battling sickness and disease. You are the Great Physician, the source of all healing and comfort. We ask for Your divine touch to be upon each suffering person, whether it is physically, emotionally, or spiritually.

Grant them the strength to endure their trials and the courage to face each day with hope and perseverance. Surround them with Your love and peace, easing their pain and comforting them in their time of need. Let Your healing power flow through their bodies, restoring them to health and wholeness according to Your will.

We also pray for the caregivers and family members who selflessly tend to the needs of their loved ones. Bless them with patience, compassion, and strength as they provide support and comfort. Grant them wisdom and guidance, and may they find rest and renewal in Your presence.

We ask all these things in Jesus' name.

Amen.

HOW MY FAITH BROUGHT ME THROUGH

September 27, 2010

It's More Than Just Hair!

Phia's hair started to fall out. As she lay in her father's arms, I was unraveling the braids to clean her hair. As I combed her hair, it became entangled with my fingers, filled the comb, and fell out on my dress and the floor. I remember when Phia was one year old, and we prayed for it to grow, and now I was putting it in a pile. Her life is more important than her hair, but it is just another thing that shows the horror of cancer.

Today, her hair was coming out in patches. As Phia drank her milk and twirled her hair with her hand, she would stop to hand me loose hair. The rest of her hair, still on top, became interlocked together. I left the two braids because I figured it was better to leave them alone, even if it gave her a day of comfort to twirl.

She started crying as she touched the places where the hair had gone. She also started pulling one of the entangled braids. The nurse said older kids said it hurt when the hair came out in clumps from the root. By 9 pm tonight, I removed the interlocked hair because she was crying and pulling at it.

That is a small thing from the perspective of what Phia has gone through and is still facing. However, the hair is the outward sign of what is happening inside. Chemo's job is to kill the bad cells and to do that, the good ones die, too.

Physically, today has been challenging for Phia. She woke with a high fever and needed a platelet transfusion. The transfusion could not take place until the fever broke. Because of the fever, the nurse had to access the other side of the port in her chest to run antibiotics through the line. (So, infection does not get within the line). As I think about updating Phia's journal, I wonder if I need to get as detailed or clinical as I do. Sometimes, I want to stop writing because it takes an emotional toll, reliving the day and emotions again.

Then I think about all the times I turned the Saint Jude commercials off because I could not take the images of the children with cancer. I purposely closed my eyes because I did not want to deal with it. But according to the stats, we should not keep our eyes closed.

In reality, one in three people will develop some type of cancer in their lifetime. There are over two hundred types of cancer. So, as I want to stop writing, I think maybe my family's trial and Sophia's battle can help someone cope with a cancer diagnosis or help others be more compassionate to those who have it. I pray.

September 30. 2010
THANK YOU, GOD!

Praise God! Keep praying because God is listening and moving! Sophia had her much-awaited MRI this morning. Hours passed before one of her team members could tell me the results. When Sophia and I were about to fall asleep, one of the neurologists popped his head into the room to discuss the MRI results. Dr. Hojay (he said the pronunciation is Yahweh. I said Yahweh as in God, and he said yes) said Sophia's MRI showed a remarkable improvement.

It was almost like the news bounced off me for a minute. I asked if it was better than September 18, but how is it compared to the one taken on September 2, when I found out the cancer spread? I wanted to find out if we reverted to our starting point or if we had progressed beyond where we were when she first diagnosed us. He could not answer that question. I had to wait for the head neurologist to come by.

A few hours later, the head neurologist and the fellow came excited about the improvement. They put all three MRIs up on the screen. It was amazing to see the dramatic improvement. It was the first time I saw the grooves of the brain because tumors filled it. The tumor on the pineal gland is a little smaller and doctors hope that the next few rounds of chemo will destroy it. The spine showed a remarkable improvement. Previously, the cancer was the length of the spinal cord, and the tumor was pushing up against it. The new MRI showed that the treatment destroyed most of the tumor.

HOW MY FAITH BROUGHT ME THROUGH

October 2, 2010

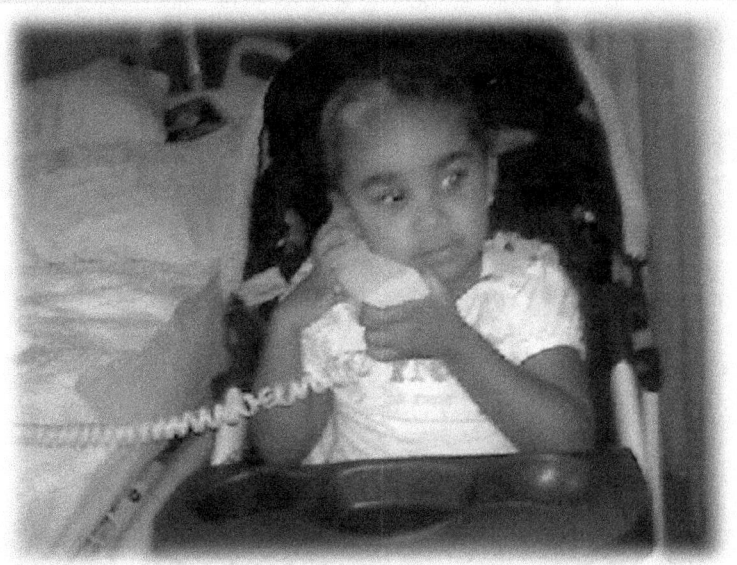

Sophia had a good day. She did not have any tests, and she had a special visit with her Abuela. Around 9 pm, she started to fall asleep. As my daughter slept, I started thinking about how God answers prayers. When I was pregnant and found out I was having a girl, one of my constant prayers was that my daughter be a better woman than me. When we ask things of God, we never have a clue how He will answer us.

Sometimes, the trials we go through and the lessons we are to learn are the very answers to our petitions. Before Sophia fell asleep, she heard her roommate, Emma, crying. Sophia started crying, and when I calmed her down, she extended her arm to the other side of the room and said, "Baby crying, mommy, baby crying."

The way she said it was like a plea for help. I began to tear up, thinking about how compassionate she was. Then I started to think about her lying in a hospital bed for seventeen straight days, and knowing she was taking this far better than I ever would. A smile crossed my face, and I thought, "Wow, God is showing me already how He heard my prayer." She is learning patience at two years old, which has taken my entire life.

Life has had to humble me through trial after trial to have the same compassion she has at two. After all, she has gone through and is going through, she can still make her father and I laugh. Sophia does not know what it is like to have a "normal" life. As babies explore their surroundings, develop, and learn, Sophia is constantly fighting from eye cancer, brain, and spinal cancer, surgery after surgery, to learning to use her legs all over again. When I think about her incredible strength, I am in awe. Someone asked me, "Why Sophia?" I answered, "Why not." I am in a hospital filled with Sophia's. Every parent on this floor loves their child as much as I love mine.

Someone else said they needed help understanding how God could let this happen to them. Honestly, I did not want to answer that question. I felt like I was going through so much now; how could I minister to someone else? Then, I had to go to the scriptures. Isaiah 55:8 says, "God's thoughts are not my thoughts; neither are your ways, my ways." How I would do something is not how God will. Just because my husband and I serve God does not mean we get a pass-free card from life. Through the trials of life and how we exercise our faith, we grow, and those around us see God's glory.

An unseen God becomes tangible. I have done more ministry during this hospital stay than all year. One of the most outstanding examples was when a nurse said she was angry with God and closed her heart to Him because of all the suffering she saw. She said that because of seeing the strength and faith of my family, her heart has softened to God again. WOW, that is nothing but HIS GLORY!

Because of this trial, there is something that all of us are to get, whether faith, hope, encouragement, strength, humility, courage, and trust. For me, it is very humbling to know that I do not get a pass-free card. This trial has shown me that life will consistently put obstacles before you to show you who you are and, more importantly, who God is. We are to depend on Him, period, the end.

October 7, 2010

No Place Like Home

Today, Sophia could feel the wind on her face for the first time in 22 days. She is now peacefully resting in our bed. We went back to the hospital on Monday for several tests. On Tuesday, Phia starts the second round of chemotherapy. Being home for the weekend will be nice—a much-needed break! Thanks for all the support, love, and well wishes. Please do not stop praying. That is only round #1; Sophia has four more to go.

October 11, 2010

It is amazing what we take for granted each day. We forget how fragile life is and how everyday there is something to be thankful for. Sophia was so excited to have socks on when we got home from the hospital. She could not walk, but kept saying, "Socks, mommy, look at my socks." I realized at that moment I was being very ungrateful.

I have fallen into the trap of looking at all that is wrong and not giving thanks for what is right. It is the small things we take for granted or overlook because they seem insignificant until something happens that shakes us up. Sometimes, life will throw you upside down to make things right.

Sunday morning, we decided to take Phia to the church. As soon as we walked into the sanctuary, Phia could not contain her excitement when she saw David, her best friend. She said, "Mommy, get out," so I laid a sheet on the floor and took her out of her stroller. She stiffened her legs in protest as I tried to put her down. She leaned on me and took a few steps. In her frustration, she started crying because her legs were not doing what she wanted. My eyes got watery because it blessed my heart to see those few steps. Later, she took a few more steps for her father.

On Monday, Sophia had a long day at the hospital. She had her hearing tested because the chemo drugs can cause hearing loss. Sophia had her kidney function tested because chemo is hard on the kidneys, liver, and lungs. She also had an ultrasound on her neck. We are still waiting for the results, but everything looks good. The blood drawn on Saturday had bacteria present. We are still waiting to see what infection/virus is detected.

October 16-21, 2010

Phia faced another health scare with bacteria in her blood, prompting urgent hospitalization and a change in antibiotics. Despite setbacks like delayed surgery and fever spikes, she underwent necessary procedures and a blood transfusion before finally returning home. However, the roller coaster of emotions continued as she battled pain and refused to eat.

Amidst the struggles, the family finds comfort in small acts of kindness and the support of hospital staff and fellow families enduring similar hardships. While our "new normal" is daunting, we remain hopeful for Phia's recovery and seek to make a difference by encouraging others to contribute in simple yet meaningful ways.

HOW MY FAITH BROUGHT ME THROUGH

October 22, 2010

A Mother's Thoughts

When I take a minute to reflect on all the things my daughter has had to endure, tears fill my eyes. Or how much her appearance has changed from the drugs that have gone through her little body. I try not to think about all the chemicals that are pumped into her body each day, week, or month. I close my eyes while holding her hand when they remove her dressing over her port or give her a shot. I'm just hoping it is over any minute so we can put it behind us.

When I look at all the black and blues on her legs from the shots she gets twice a day, I tell myself this is the price she has to pay to save her life. I tell myself tomorrow is not promised to any of us to comfort my heart when I have moments of what ifs. I hold onto every laugh or smile she makes, almost like I'm trying to memorize or caption it. I try not to look at pictures from just a few months ago so my mind does not live in the past or get trapped there.

I find it harder and harder each time I push Phia in her stroller past the school playground near the hospital. The children run and laugh while I put my daughter in her stroller because she cannot walk yet. She watches the kids with a longing in her eyes. Or when my heart sinks when they look at her, trying to figure out why she does not have hair.

At those moments, I realized there was a difference between the other children and Sophia. It seems that while we were held up in the hospital room, the world goes on. I find myself drawing closer to the parents of the children on the pediatric floor, not just because of the common bond, but because I feel awkward around those who do not have to face this kind of trial. Just doing our daily routines feels strange. When I get a moment to get away, I bump into someone who does not know what we are going through, and they ask me about Phia. When I try to brush past what is going on, I get a look of pity for my family and me.

Even when I went to church one Sunday and Juan was with Phia, I felt such an emptiness that my family was not together. I try not to think about tomorrow as much anymore. Or when people get tired of hearing about our struggles. I have been trying to focus on what to be thankful for. Seeing Phia each day, I am grateful for the breath in her body. I am thankful for those around her who help care for her. I am pleased that we did not have to get uprooted or travel from one part of the country to visit NY for treatment. I am grateful for seeing her smile and laugh. I am thankful for so much.

I was able to leave the hospital tonight and go home while Juan takes the night shift with Phia. Juan called, informing me that she had another fever and was crying in pain. I sat here, realizing that I may physically leave the hospital, but not in my heart. So, I try to do what I can while I am home to keep my household moving forward.

I tell myself this will be behind us one day, and something great must come from this. So, as I drop to my knees in prayer tonight, I will thank God and ask for his continued mercy on my family and that He bless all those who have been a blessing to us.

October 25, 2010

Blood Donors Save Lives!

Phia went to the blood donor room at the cancer hospital to have her stem cells harvested. Before they hooked Phia up to the machine to harvest her cells, they had to prime the machine with donor blood because of her size. The nurse then hooked her lines (tubes) to the machine tubes. Phia's blood then goes from the port in her chest into the apheresis machine, where the stem cells are separated, and the remaining blood is sent back into the port in her chest. The process took 3 hours, but due to the problems with her lines and the prep, we were at the hospital for 8 *hours. The hospital called to inform me that they had more than enough stem cells, so she will not need to return tomorrow! Praise God! Praise God! Praise God!*

October 28, 2010

Today, Phia had her kidneys and hearing checked. Praise God, the test came back fine. It is 2:30 am, and I cannot sleep. I must write my feelings, so my daughter understands what she had to endure and overcome. The pain and suffering were for a greater purpose, and her life impacted on those around her.

The longer I live and think I have finally arrived, the more I realize how much further I must go. Life has a way of humbling you through the progress of each trial. These are things you never thought you could do, would do, or should do as a parent or caregiver. When I had dreams of marriage and children, I never thought I would spend the first two years of my daughter's life in and out of hospitals. I never thought I would have to endure the pain of watching my baby suffer. Or, having to comfort my son as he feared the possibility of losing his sister.

Through it all, I have learned invaluable lessons that only going through the fire can bring. Since my daughter has been diagnosed with cancer, I have seen the best and worst in people. I have seen a level of selfishness that is disturbing and a level of selflessness that is inspiring. I have seen blessings come from places I would have never thought of. I have seen the kindness of strangers and the avoidance of some who cannot deal with a child being ill. I have learned that everyone handles tragic events differently, but that does not mean their pain is any less because they do not wear it on their sleeve.

I have learned to move into action and try to do something instead of saying, "Let me know if you need anything." Most people will not say what they need because they are overwhelmed or do not want to impose. I have seen the non-believers show more spiritual maturity than I (a faithful churchgoer) by not questioning God why their child is ill. I have realized that having faith does not mean you do not have moments where fear tries to overtake you, or you do not feel the pain of the trial.

Saints seem to forget that even Jesus cried tears of blood. I have realized that saying you trust God when you feel a sense of control is not trusting Him. It is not until you feel like you are spinning out of control that you realize how much you need to trust God more. I have learned that I cannot control life, but all I can do is try not to let the struggles of life control me.

I can choose to find joy each day, not wallow in self-pity. I can be thankful and believe all this works for my family's "good." I can live in the moment, not in the what-ifs of tomorrow. I have seen how Sophia Nicole Roman's life for two years has made a difference. For one, her life has gotten countless people praying from all walks of life.

HOW MY FAITH BROUGHT ME THROUGH

October 30, 2010

HOW DO YOU SEE IT

Around 3 am, Phia started crying for a bottle. I told her I could not give her milk, but I could give her apple juice or water. In the past, Phia would cry more after I said those words because she knew that meant we were going to the hospital for a test (she is allowed clear liquids up to 2 hours before anesthesia). This time, Phia paused and said, "Juice mommy," because she knew I would not give her that after a while, and something was better than nothing.

It amazes me how we learn valuable life lessons at such a young age. So, a few hours later, I dressed in the dark and put her stuff in the car while she slept. We packed *the car by 6:30 am for Phia's 7:30 am MRI tests. Thank God, there was little wait time before they came for Phia today. The anesthesiologist told me they would bring her upstairs afterward for her "procedure." I did not know what he was talking about, and he seemed confused that I did not either.*

I removed Phia's earrings and held her in my arms while they administered the anesthesia. That way, she does not freak out for a few minutes while lying on the stretcher, not knowing what will happen to her. I laid her down until she was knocked out, and immediately went upstairs to find out what procedure the anesthesiologist was talking about.

The image of countless tales where individuals enter hospitals for one reason, only to have doctors inadvertently remove a limb or organ, surged through my mind. The nurse practitioner apologized that no one told me she had a spinal tap scheduled. But since no one told me about it and I had to give her a blood thinner shot, they could not do that additional procedure. Once again, the hospital showed me that things fall through the cracks, and I cannot let down my guard for a minute to ensure the safety of my daughter.

It took three hours to do an MRV of the veins of the brain and neck and an MRI of the brain and the spine. It took another three hours of waiting for the results. After my patience was exhausted, I told them to call me with the results.

A few hours later, I got a call from the resident Oncologist. He explained the mixed results. There was improvement with the cancer layers on the sides of the brain. The tumor in the brain and the cancer of the spine remained stable.

While Juan, Domonick, and I listened in our car while on the speaker, we were all quiet. I did not even hear any of us breathing. Dom kept on drawing while waiting to get cues from us. Juan was listening to hear God, knowing I was soaking in what the doctor just said. Of course, Phia was babbling up a storm, bouncing off our silence.

My mind was battling whether we made the right decision by removing one of the chemo drugs from the last cycle. The drug is known to cause hearing damage, and we did not want to continue to use it because Phia already has vision impairment issues. I felt like I had let her down. I did not know how to take the information I just heard.

Then I asked if she still had the blood clot in her neck and learned it was stable. Right then, a massive wave of discouragement washes over me. We were hoping and praying the blood clot would break up because we have been giving her blood thinner shots twice a day in her legs at home. Giving her these shots is getting harder and harder. To where I can hardly look in her eyes while we put the needle into her leg. I see such fear in her eyes as she screams "Mommy no" or "Daddy no, no, and no" while she shakes, trembles, kicks, and fights us... She freaks out before and after. This scene plays out mildly while we try to change her diaper because she thinks we are trying to give her another shot. We tell her over and over again that we are just changing her diaper. So, as I thought about all this playing out, I paused for so long that the doctor interjected, asking me if I was crying.

I said no, just taking it all in. So, we have to go back in on Monday for the spinal tap. On Wednesday, we will talk to the head of the team about how we will proceed with the next round of chemo, which should start on Thursday. I was blessed tonight to see Phia hold onto Juan's hand and walk from our hallway through the living room into the dining room. It was fifteen feet, but it was like she ran a 5k race and came in first place. I cried tears of joy. I was so thankful God strengthened her to encourage us tonight. My heart is overjoyed with gladness!

I decided to see her MRI results in a positive light. I hoped for the destruction of all the cancer cells, but I will *rejoice in the improvement on the sides of her brain, and the cancer not progressing in the other areas. I have been guilty of not celebrating and thanking God for the milestone blessings. But I am consciously choosing to see the glass half full this time. For those who know me, that is a victory right there in itself.*

November 5, 2010

Bed seventeen is where Phia has been getting chemotherapy administered in the day hospital for two days. She is doing as well as expected. Phia got sick several times last night and this morning due to the drugs. The neurologist stopped by and was amazed by Phia's progress with her walking. A month ago, their team informed us that it could take up to a year before she could walk unrestricted. Within three weeks, Phia got back feeling in both legs, applied pressure on both, and started walking by holding onto someone or something for short periods. The resident neurologist who visited from Canada said he was glad he saw Sophia's progress. He said he could inform other parents in similar situations that it would be possible to have great results quickly. He acknowledged that prayer played a big part in it! We are waiting for the nurse to transfer us to the inpatient area, where Sophia will be for the next few days, because the hospital is closed over the weekend.

November 8, 2010
Prayers Are Working!

Phia amazes me. We came home with a backpack of fluids attached to a tube in her chest. (It weighs about twenty pounds) That did not stop her from trying to walk and be mobile. I placed the backpack in her shopping cart, and she pushed it around the house. She walked up the stairs today (while I stood behind her carrying the pack) and walked a few feet without leaning onto anything! Phia keeps surpassing the doctor's expectations. She is truly a fighter! Phia has lost almost all the steroid weight. Her face has thinned back to where it was before we found out the cancer had spread. Phia is still two pounds lighter than when she first went into the hospital in September. Because of the sores in her mouth and her being nauseous from the chemo, Phia has not been eating or holding things down. Prayerfully, she can get a few weeks of eating in before we start the fourth round of chemo.

Please keep praying for her strength! We have been told that the Chemo rounds she just completed were the easiest part in comparison to conclusion phase (fifth

HOW MY FAITH BROUGHT ME THROUGH

round). During this round, she will have to be in isolation and hospitalized for 4 to 6 weeks.

On November 11, 2010, my journal entry was a plea for all prayer warriors to intercede on behalf of Sophia, receiving a miraculous move by God. Since September, we have been administering blood thinner shots twice a day to address a blood clot in her vein. Witnessing the physical toll it has taken on her tiny body, marked by bruises and fear, is heart-wrenching. The emotional strain on us as parents is immense despite understanding it is for her well-being.

Despite medical advice, we believe in God's ultimate authority over Sophia's health. We pray fervently for the clot to dissolve before the upcoming ultrasound. Additionally, I request prayers for her mouth infection to heal and for her body to withstand the challenges of chemotherapy.

November 25, 2010

Enter his gates with thanksgiving and his courts with praise; give thanks to him and praise his name. For the LORD is good and his love endures forever; his faithfulness continues through all generations.
Psalm 100:4-5 (NIV)

We have so much to be thankful for this day, for what the Lord has done! Matthew 21:22 says, "Whatever things you ask in prayer, believing, you will receive." Yesterday, Sophia had a battery of tests taken to see if the last round of chemotherapy had any adverse effects on her kidneys and hearing. I am still waiting for the kidney test, but I am thankful to report that her hearing has not been affected.

HOW MY FAITH BROUGHT ME THROUGH

A week and a half ago, I asked one of her team members to schedule an ultrasound so we could see if the clot in her jugular vein had broken up. Politely, the doctor told me the chance of it breaking up was slim and that a person could be on blood thinners for up to six months before it breaks up. I told the nurse that my Bible says God is an ever-present help in a time of trouble! My husband and I cannot bear giving our baby shots twice a day anymore. I said my God is faithful to his Word and we would call on my prayer warriors to intercede for God to move. I am overjoyed to say God heard and moved in Phia's favor.

The vein is flowing unrestricted. When I told the same team member, they looked at me with shock. The team member said, "I know you did not doubt it," but Sophia just had an MRV three weeks ago, and it was still there.

Then, she said, "I need to give you a list of children to pray for!" To God be the glory.

I have not yet talked to the head of the team, but the unofficial recommendation is to continue the shots until she has another MRV (which is like an MRI but of the veins). Usually, once the clot is gone, they recommend continuing the shots for up to 6 months. But I believe God will let us know when discontinuing is safe. I prayed God would not allow the ultrasound to happen unless it showed us favorable results.

I stand in awe today. God knows He heard our cry because of His love and mercy. He keeps showing me that He is faithful. In sixty-six books that make up the Bible, it does not say once that we will not go through trials. But it does say He will be with you when you do. He will strengthen, comfort, carry, and even hide you behind his shadow. I am glad to know Him, and I give him thanks on this Thanksgiving Day! Thank you all for your prayers! Be encouraged that God hears you too! Happy Turkey Day! Continue to thank Him for those things you have not seen yet and watch Him move on your behalf!

December 4, 2010

It's A Part of The Process

This week, Sophia finished her fourth round of chemo. We were in the day hospital for four days to receive medicine and fluids. As soon as her body recovers from the last round, another begins. After two weeks of trying to get her to eat and drink around Thanksgiving, she was in a good place.

When I brought Sophia to the hospital this past Tuesday, my heart was heavy. As she laughed and played with me in the hospital bed, I thought in just a few hours, her body would feel sick. I must keep telling myself that we are pumping poison into her body to save her life. As Sophia looks into my eyes, I whisper to her that I am sorry. I find myself saying that to her a lot. "Mommy's sorry." Sorry that she must go through this, sad that I have to allow it. I am sorry that she does not understand all that she is going through.

On the ride home, Sophia starts crying and gets sick while I drive. So, with one hand on the stirring wheel and the other trying to push her forward so she does not choke, I managed to pull over. I frantically get out of the car to clean her up and strip her clothes while the wind whips in the vehicle. Sophia shivers, and those same eyes look at me, wondering why this is happening. This scene plays out for the next three days, going to and leaving the hospital.

Despite not eating in three days and having extreme nausea during the day, Phia was playing in the hospital playroom. I am amazed at her strength and resilience in not letting the sickness stop her. Even in her bed of affliction, she continues to show a level of compassion that is inspiring. She heard a baby crying and said, "Mommy baby crying," then, "I want to see the baby." Before we left, I asked them to run her blood counts, but the doctor *did not order it. I insisted I wanted the test anyway. The nurse came in and said, "A mother knows." Phia's white blood cell counts were dropping quickly. So, we were able to give her a shot to help boost the level or at least to keep it stable. We must be back on Monday for a possible blood transfusion. Please continue to pray for Phia's strength and her body's ability to bounce back quickly.*

December 17, 2010

Give Life

    Since the last round of Chemo, Sophia's body has been on the rebound. She has needed two blood transfusions and a platelet transfusion. Since September, she has had about ten transfusions. When I gave blood in the past, I never thought about cancer patients needing transfusions. I felt that it went to people who had horrible accidents, surgery, or Hemophiliacs.

As I went through the process of giving blood, I reminded myself that one pint could make the difference between life and death. I never really thought that all those times I donated, I would one day be on the receiving end, let alone my child. Ten anonymous people have given my daughter the gift of life. A simple selfless act keeps my daughter's body fighting with the constant assault of chemo. I cannot thank the ten people who took the time out of their busy schedules to make a difference in a little girl's life they do not even know. But I am charged to keep giving blood.

I cannot give it to my daughter because we are incompatible, but I can give the gift to another family. Blood Banks rely on family members and friends of patients and people who live and work in the community to maintain an adequate supply of blood to support the transfusion needs of their patients. Giving blood takes up to 10 minutes. Platelet donation takes longer to deliver, about two and ½ hours. When platelet levels fall too low, patients' blood cannot clot. Some patients, especially those who have had a bone marrow transplant or who are treated for leukemia, may require daily platelet transfusions for several weeks.

So, if you want to give the gift of life this holiday season, please make an appointment at your local blood bank.

Be blessed and continue to be a blessing!

December 21, 2010

Love in Action

There are no words to express the level of gratitude that I have this holiday season. Every time I fasted and prayed; God asked me what I wanted. The answer has always been my daughter's complete healing and restoration of her body, and that I would see her grow up to be a remarkable woman of God. I have never wanted something more in my entire life.

All I thought about for a long time was the "what ifs." The fear of not getting my heart's desire gripped me with such fear. I would often think, if it were not God's will to heal my daughter, how would my heart recover? I then had to pray off the fear because it was choking the life out of my faith and hope for a mighty move from God.

Whenever God moved in Sophia's favor, I was afraid to rejoice because I feared another setback. All I was doing was robbing God of His glory. Fear was stopping me from rejoicing in the milestone blessings. My heart is overflowing with thanksgiving today. My daughter has gotten her appetite back. Sophia is running through the house even though the doctors said it could have taken her a year to do that. Phia is learning more words, and she has started to play dress-up.

Whenever she says, "Mommy, look," I smile to see what she is doing. Yesterday, she put a small blanket on her head with a hat and walked around the room. Sophia looked like "cousin Itt" from the Addams Family. I could not stop laughing. Having no hair does not stop her from believing she has some.

What I cherish the most is holding her hand and feeling the warmth of it. I am also grateful for the generosity shown to my family through gifts, notes, and acts of kindness. I'm so thankful for the endless prayers that have gone up for our family. To the kind words posted to me. Thank you all for putting love into action. That is the meaning behind the birth of Jesus, Love.

Merry Christmas and happy holidays to all!

Be Blessed and Continue to be a Blessing!

CHAPTER 8
Battling the Beast

January 4, 2011

The Cost of Her Praise

We celebrated the incoming of the New Year in fellowshipping at another church. Sophia took center stage, dancing, and singing in the aisle. Everyone was watching this two-year-old throw her hands in the air, shook her shoulders and hips and moving her feet to the beat. An older man came up to me and said it was a blessing to see her so excited to praise God. With a heavy heart, I responded, "If only you knew what it cost her to offer that praise."

This courageous little girl has been fighting advanced cancer in her spine, which left her paralyzed for some time. The illness then spread to her brain, causing seizures, and endangering her eyesight. That prompts *doctors to consider eye removal—a measure we declined because God said no.*

She was singing to God and dancing because even at two, she knew what God did for her. I watched and was amazed how she has not let any of her trials get her down.

Earlier that day, a friend of Sophia's grandfather passed away. This friend made it to my father's funeral service and told me she had to hold Sophia. She had to hold the miracle of God. She felt strengthened and encouraged by her. That is God's Glory! Such is the power of God's glory—often mysterious, yet always revealing itself in times of need.

Phia's strength has unknowingly become a beacon of hope for many. That week, we awaited her latest test results with anticipation. Before beginning her final round of chemotherapy—a high dose intended to eliminate the cancer—she underwent a series of tests to assess her resilience and the extent of the disease. So far, MRI scans have shown no progression since the previous treatment, with doctor's hopeful that the detected masses were calcified (dead cells).

However, when tests confirmed the presence of active cancer cells in her spinal fluid, it dampened our optimism. This news was disheartening, especially after being informed that Sophia was facing a more advanced stage of the disease compared to other patients in this treatment phase. I hold on to my faith because, although I yearn for the doctors to declare that she is surpassing expectations, any mother in my shoes just wants to hear that her baby will beat this.

My fear of the drugs affecting her hearing came to pass. The hearing test showed that Sophia had hearing loss in her high pitch frequency hearing. This does not affect her everyday hearing or hearing for normal speech development. It affects her ability to hear certain high pitch sounds in very loud environments. The doctor said that this is a permanent loss. The hearing test hit me hard...the realization to save her life comes with a cost sent my thoughts racing.

Even though it does not affect everyday hearing it is another thing that the cancer stole from Sophia. The cost that has to be added up is how much of her quality of life will be affected? Before we start the mega round, we have some hard decisions to make. The one drug they use can possibly cause more hearing loss. The weight of that decision had me pull the covers over my head and go to sleep when I got home. Sometimes it hits me, that this is life or death. I do not see it that way on a day-to-day basis. You cannot because the realization of that would cause you to stay in depression, or not move out of fear. Prior to this last round "the Mega dose" round, this cancer has been fatal. With its patients have a 30 to 40 percent chance to live cancer free lives. So, parents hope and pray that their child will be one of the lucky ones. I do not believe in luck. I believe in God.

This is where I put my trust. So, I have to trust God has Sophia in the palm of His hands during all of this. Her Kidney test came back fine. They gave me a card to carry in my wallet in case homeland security stops me...wow. To take the test, they put an IV in Sophia's arm to then put radioactive substance into her vein... The test is called a kidney nuclear medicine scan; it is to reveal how the kidneys are functioning. When I think how I would not even take an aspirin when I was pregnant in fear of harming the baby...and now they are pumping radioactive nuclear substance, chemo drugs, etc. into my daughter, it is beyond disturbing.

Everything you know and fear must be dismissed to move forward to fight this disease. Phia has to have a heart test and an MRV (test of the veins of the head and neck) before her last round starts. The last round is scheduled to start next Monday. Please keep Phia in your prayers. Pray that her body recovers quickly. Pray for our strength because this last round will have her hospitalized in isolation for 4 to 6 weeks. That means no leaving that room for over a month. Phia is going from 10 hours of Chemo to 36 hours. This round will whip out her bone marrow. After six days of chemo, she will get two days of fluids and then she will get her stem cells back. This is called the recovery phase, which takes the longest because the body has to recover. Children usually do not eat for 2 weeks and must be on pain killers because of the soars in the mouth. I look forward to the day that all of this is a memory. I look forward to the day that Sophia can recapture the carefree days of childhood. I look forward to seeing her grow older. I do not take for granted one moment. Every time I see Sophia play, laugh, or smile I watch with eyes of gladness. I close my eyes and I say thank you for that moment.

January 21, 2011

Phia's Room at Hospital Day 4. Because of cold and flu season, Sophia's isolation started today. When she realized we could not leave the room, she threw her body in front of the door and started kicking and screaming. Thank God shortly after that outburst; she had several visits back-to-back. Sophia had a session with the dance and music therapists and a visit from a child life representative.

I then picked her up and she stood looking out the window for a while. It is crazy how much cancer steals *from you. Now it has taken her freedom to come and go. For her safety my daughter must be closed off from everything she loves and tucked away into a room. To Sophia this room is a cell and she has been wrongly convicted. She does not understand why she is here and more importantly why she cannot go home.*

Since we have been coming to the hospital Sophia has had a pretty good attitude despite it all. Watching her for the past few days we have seen glimpses of a little girl who is sad. My heart ached when she got quiet and put her head down and said in a whisper, "I want to go home." When it is time for Juan and Dom to go home, Sophia starts screaming knowing she is not leaving with them. Then for an hour afterwards she keeps asking me where they are. I tell her this is only for a little while. I tell her that this is to get her better. I tell her or should I say I tell myself this time will go by quickly, let us just make the best of it. Anyone who comes into the room must put on an isolation robe, mask, wash their hands, and glove up. It was a lot for Sophia at first. She did not understand why everyone was dressed that way. Especially her own mom; I had to wear a mask at all times. I did not realize how much I kissed Sophia each day when I cannot do it. So, I kiss her through the mask or pull it up and kiss the top of her head. For three days she has received chemo. Sophia has not really eaten since we came to the hospital on Tuesday. At first it was her nerves, now it is out of fear of throwing up. Today I see dark circles under her eyes that seem to have appeared overnight. Sophia's energy level is decreasing but she still wants to play.

As Phia sleeps right now, I let out the tears that I could not release in front of her. Tears from seeing her suffer and not being able to fix it. Knowing it is going to get worse before it gets better. Wondering how this is affecting her mental health. Understanding is a part of the process, and it is something else we have to get through. The weight of the glory...is the going through part. "When His glory shall be revealed, ye may be glad also with exceeding joy." (Glory is the manifestation part...in this case its Sophia's healing.)

January 24, 2011

10 days in, yet it is counted as Zero. The past two days Phia has been pretty out of it. Tuesday was the first time since she got sick that she had absolutely no play in her. It was very hard to look into her eyes because you saw a little girl who got knocked down and did not have the strength to get up. You saw the pain and discomfort Sophia felt and the sadness beneath it. She slept most of Tuesday and a large part of Wednesday.

Sophia was itchy early Wednesday morning; they think from the residue of the drugs working out of her. For her to go back to sleep I had to give her a sponge bath. She sat up to play later in the day. Her favorite thing right now is putting puffy stickers on paper and peeling them off and putting them back on. She also plays with a toy syringe. She actually sleeps with it in her hand like it is a stuff animal. Only my kid. She also played today with a tiara and jewelry our friends set her. She ate a little food today but then threw it up hours later. She was finally resting at 1:30 am.

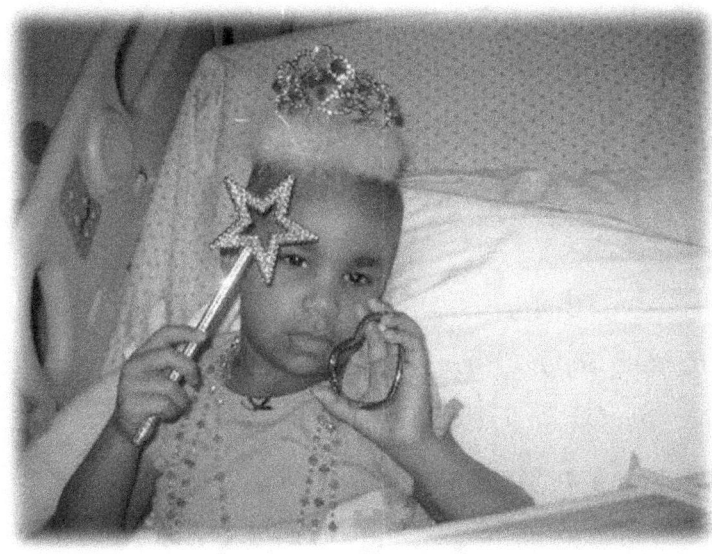

In several hours Sophia will have her transplant. Today is day ten in the hospital but the doctors call today ground zero. One nurse said to me that today is Sophia's new birthday because she got her transplant. Everyone is making a big deal but from what I am told it is uneventful. It is like getting blood or platelets transfusion. Sophia's stems cells are in a bag of blood hooked up the same way as a transfusion. I just pray that she does not have any side effects and that she heals quicker than expected. Sophia wants to go home, and we want her there.

January 29, 2011

Day 2 After Transplant Day 12 In the Hospital. Yesterday, Sophia's transplant took about 10 minutes. The doctor had a huge syringe filled with 8,000,000 flittered stem cells that were harvested from Sophia in November. The doctor twisted the syringe onto the tube that runs into her port and just slowly pushed the fluid into her body.

Sophia woke up crying because she had three doctors holding her arms and body in position. One doctor also said she probably tasted the solution of the stem cells in her mouth.

As Phia's white blood cells had dropped, she had gotten thrush in the mouth. The doctor said that she has the beginning of mucositis forming in the mouth. Let us pray that the mouth sores do not form. Chemotherapy-induced mucositis is the inflammation of your mucous membranes, which are tissues that line your digestive system – all the way from your mouth, esophagus, stomach, intestines, rectum to your anus. Mucositis is caused when chemotherapy attacks and kills the rapidly dividing cells in your mucous membranes. This condition feels like sunburn (or heartburn) on your mucous tissues, and often leads to sores in your mouth or on your tongue.

This morning Phia needed a platelet transfusion. and the doctors are starting her on Total Parenteral Nutrition (TPN). Basically, she is going to get nutrition through a tube in her chest since she is not really eating. The TPN may include a combination of sugar and carbohydrates, proteins, lipids, electrolytes, and trace elements. Phia has been doing better. The chemo may have knocked her down, but she did not stay down, she has gotten her play back. She gets tired quickly but after a nap wants to play some more.

January 30, 2011

THANK YOU ALL

During this two-year ordeal I have seen something that would break the strongest person down; through my daughter's struggles and those who carry the burden of this terrible disease. I have seen the worst in people's selfishness and the best in the generosity of people's hearts. It is like a flower that grew from concrete. The concrete is this cancer and the flower is all the beautiful things I have witnessed through this trial. From the generosity of strangers, to loved ones sacrificing their time to come to our aid. The meals cooked with love to lift the burden. To people who I have not seen in years sending my daughter care packages. To people being inspired by Sophia to give blood or volunteer at a local hospital.

Donations, words of encouragement, to the countless outpours of acts of love and compassion have overwhelmed my heart. Sometimes you must go through the fire to appreciate what is around you. I needed to see the good in people again. I needed to see the generosity of other's hearts. The bible says do not get weary in well doing, but I had. Those who truly know me know that I have the anointing to give. I love to give and when I cannot it does something inside of me. But giving for so long, I needed to be on the other end. Reminds me when God said to Elijah there are 7,000 others who have not worshipped Baal. See Elijah thought he was the only one left. The only one still serving God but just because he did not see it, it did not mean they did not exist.

I needed to see there were others who give from the heart. Others who give out of their own need. I needed to see others moved to compassion and show acts of kindness. Seeing it has replenished me and enabled me to see clearly again. This in turn has helped me to trust God more. We have been placed in a position where we must trust God to provide for our daily needs (which He has, and it blows our minds). We must trust Him for us to keep helping others even when we are in need ourselves.

We must trust Him in our daughters' healing despite the odds. We have to trust that He will bring us through this, and we will get to the other side better and stronger. Knowing that Sophia is an inspiration and a catalyst for prayer is truly a gift. We find comfort in knowing her struggles and ours as a family is not in vain.

I pray that when you read these posts, it makes you stop for a moment in your busy day to count your blessings. That it makes you appreciate those who you have in your life, your health and that it brings you and your family closer and fills your hearts with gratitude. As I walked outside this morning and saw our former neighbor shoveling our driveway, it moved me to tears. I was inspired to write this as tears rolled down uncontrollably. I am so overwhelmed by all the acts of love, and all I can say is Thank You. I pray that God blesses all of you for looking after one of His own.

February 2, 2011
DON'T MESS WITH TUBIE OR WIPIE!

All the side effects Sophia is experiencing are from the mega dose of Chemo. Chemo is no joke. Phia skin has darkened several shades, even more in some areas. Her nail beds have also darkened. Sophia has burn looking marks where her bandage was from the drug that had to be washed after administered. The burns are like sunburns, and it is very itchy. Each day the doctors have been upping her pain medicine, which helps. She will most likely need another blood transfusion today or tomorrow.

Sophia is finding comfort from her toy syringe. She calls it her "tubie." She will not let it out of her sight. She holds it all day, sleeps with it and even takes it into the bath. For the past two days Sophia had been holding in her other hand an individually packaged alcohol prep pad, which she calls her "wipie." She woke up and the first thing she said was, "Mommy where is my wipie?" The wipe happened to drop out of her hand when she was sleeping. We have to pry both things out of her hands because she is holding on so hard.

That tells a story all by itself. Other kids have a favorite blanket or stuffed animal, but that is not Sophia's normal. Sophia's normal is hospitals, doctors, nurses, tubes, syringes, medicine, alcohol pads to clean her tubes, etc. Here is to the day her normal will tell the story of a happy healthy little girl.

February 2, 2010

17 days in the hospital so far and 7 days after transplant. Today was a good day for Sophia. Less stuff was coming up and they increased her pain meds again. This enabled her to have dance therapy and physical therapy. The nurse had to make a line change, so Phia was detached from all her medicines and fluids for an hour. For

about ten minutes, I held Sophia's hand as she got her balance, as we tried to run around the room. She took a bath and then sat by the door and watched people walk by. Sophia was happy when people saw her sitting at the window at the door and said something through the glass to her.

Sophia drew pictures for her friend from the Child Life Department and one for Titi Jenice when she stopped by for a visit. Her biggest smile and laugh came when she bounced up and down on the exercise ball during physical therapy. She had a few "moments" today but overall, it was a blessed day. I know, that I know, that I know, this was the work of God behind the scenes! Thank You, I appreciate it and truly needed it!

HOW MY FAITH BROUGHT ME THROUGH

February 14, 2010
28 Days and Counting

Each day Sophia's counts get better. She still is not really eating but they stopped the nutrition bag completely in hopes of generating an appetite. Sophia has increased drinking more fluids. Her medicine pole has been reduced by half, praise God! She is getting more and more restless. The doctors are hopeful that Sophia will be discharged this week. She asked me to go home today. I told her soon. Then Sophia said Elmo wanted to go home. It is time...

February 15, 2011

Twenty-nine is Divine. I was going to write twenty-nine is the magic number, but magic did not have a thing to do with this blessing! Thank you, God! After 29 days in the hospital Phia was discharged! Sophia has beaten the record for the quickest transplant patient in her age group to be released 19 days after transplant. The previous record was three weeks and three days. Phia came in 5 days under that record.

I love that it is five! Five represents the number of Grace. Grace is the unmerited favor of God. It is kindness from God we do not deserve. There is nothing we have not done, nor can ever do to earn this favor. It is a gift from

God. It is God's gift that Sophia can walk out of the hospital let alone is still with us.

When the cancer spread to her brain and spine in September, it shook us to our knees. Then within two weeks it progressed so much it tripled in size. Honestly fear gripped me, and I felt like I was suffocating under it. But God chose to show His power through Sophia. Not because He loved us more, not because we deserve it but just because of His grace. Some say favor is not fair, but I am so glad we have God's favor in this situation. Through Sophia's trials, God has shown us that when we speak and pray His Word, we are coming into agreement with Him and His power is released to answer our prayers. Early today when I got the official word that we were being released I could not contain my excitement. I was skipping through the halls.

As I was packing up Sophia's room there were young people outside my door crying. It was more than just the stress of having a loved one in the hospital. I came to find out a teenage boy two doors down from me had just passed away. My heart was grieved, and I could not contain the flood of emotion. I cried like it was my child. I cried because his family did not get the miracle for which they were hoping. I broke down outside. This young boy's death humbled me. I felt humbled because now I really understood the gift that God gave me today! I did not leave skipping, or cracking lighthearted jokes, or boasting about God flexing for us today. I left quietly pushing my daughter in her stroller knowing God did not have to do this...

When we got home Sophia did not know what to do with herself first. I was pulling stuff out of a box that friends of ours sent for her. Sophia was playing musical instruments for a moment, held the white and red dog, stared at her new Barbie, looked at the cards from the kindergarten class made for her. Sophia then walked into the kitchen, sat in her highchair, and drank her water. Phia had the look on her face like I was finally home, it is real.

March 9, 2011
HALLELUJAH! NEGATIVE IS A POSITIVE THING!

The past 2 weeks Sophia had her follow up tests from the last round of Chemo. Last week she had an MRI that showed little improvement. It was the professional opinion that the tumor and layers were calcified (dead cancer cells) and/or scar tissue present instead of live cancer cells. But there was no way of knowing for sure until she had a Lumbar Puncture test (test the spinal fluid for cancer cells).

I am overjoyed and so thankful to God to report yesterday the results came in from the Lumbar Test. The report read: Cerebrospinal Fluid, Negative for Malignant Cells! In other words, God said take that cancer! Yesterday was the first time since August that Sophia had her eyes checked for cancer. It felt strange to go back to the second floor of the hospital since the cancer had spread. Strange because I had not heard from the doctor that originally treated Sophia before the cancer spread to the brain and spine. Sophia was treated by him every six weeks from 6 months old until she turned 2 years old.

It also felt strange because, before Sophia's cancer spread the parents and I would talk and trade stories in the waiting room about our children's treatment and stage of *disease. But I knew that not one of those parents waiting yesterday wanted to hear about what they feared the most. Phia puts a face on the 3% whose cancer spreads from the eyes to the brain. Most of the kids with cancer of the eyes it is about saving the eyes and not saving the life. I talked to one of the grandmothers of a boy I wrote about a long time ago who had to have his eye removed. She asked why she had not seen us in a long time and when I told her briefly, she looked horrified.*

While the nurses were waiting for Phia to wake after anesthesia I talked to the doctors. Hallelujah, the exam showed that Phia's left retina has completely reattached! Also, the three seeds in her left eye that we were treating for a year and a half before the cancer spread are finally destroyed! I do not take her results lightly. The amount of cancer Phia had its only Jehovah Rophe ("The Lord Heals") that she is still here and doing as well as she is.

May 10, 2011

Fear you not, stand still, and see the salvation of the LORD! Ex 14:13

It has been about two months since I last wrote an entry. Within these two months we have been enjoying watching our daughter gain back some normalcy in her life. Sophia no longer sleeps with a syringe in her hand or wakes up screaming in the middle of the night. The tubes are no longer hanging from her chest and her hair has grown to about a half an inch.

Sophia has gained more strength in her legs and her balance. She is able to climb up the ladder on the slide at the park like any other kid her age. Throughout the day I find myself kissing her repeatedly. I say it is time for a kiss attack and she giggles. When I do it, I silently close my eyes and feel her hair on my lips as if to know this moment is real. I then whisper, "Thank you God," as Sophia runs in front of me excited to go from one room to the other.

I have moments where thanksgiving overtakes me because I remember where she was and see where she is now. Since her last round of tests, we have been dealing with the "what's next" in treatment conversations with the doctors. The protocol from her oncology team would be to do radiation. We have had meetings with several doctors to *discuss all options. The recommendation originally was to do radiation beams to her brain and spine.*

The feeling was that a cancer cell could still be alive but undetected and doing the radiation would ensure a complete recovery. This option sickened me. A mask would have been made for her head, then Sophia would have been put under anesthesia, and then the mask would be bolted to the table so she would not move during the beaming process. Sophia would have had to do this every day for six weeks.

The risk would be a 50% change of secondary cancer forming and her IQ dropping by at least ten points. The risk of learning disabilities was great. We opted to try to do radioactive antibodies medicine through the shunt in her head. The only side effect would be a headache for 24 hours and she would only have to have the medicine administered once a week for 5 weeks.

Phia had a test done where they put dye in her shunt to see if it flowed from her brain to the spine before the actual medicine would be given. However, the dye did not move like the doctors hoped for. This hit me hard because what seemed like the best option was not working. Then I met with the surgeon who put in the shunt in her head. He felt the best option was to have surgery. He recommended drilling a hole on the opposite side of Sophia's head to then try to bypass the tumor blockage that is blocking the natural fluid flow so the antibodies would be able to travel to the spine.

Back in September he tried to avoid putting a shunt in by trying to bypass the tumor but there were thick cancer cells over the area which made it too dangerous to do. He was confident that the layer was gone, and he was able to successfully bypass the flow. He would also take a piece of tissue from the mass to make sure it was dead. This sent me into a depression for a few days. I could not stop crying. Nothing came easy in this trial and now another thing! I was not afraid of the surgery, but I could not have another hole drilled in my baby's head.

I hit that wall where I could not have another discussion, nor could I go through another thing. The doctors kept trying to pressure me to move and I said not until God speaks, I am not moving ahead of Him. Throughout this trial I have had to make decisions that I did not like but I knew it was what needed to be done. This go around I did not feel either choice was the right one. So, Juan and I prayed, prayed, and prayed some more. God spoke, "He said for Sophia to have another MRI, and we would know how to move from there."

HOW MY FAITH BROUGHT ME THROUGH

I told the doctors what God said. We just had an MRI a month after the last round of chemo, so no one was expecting it to be a big difference either way. The MRI showed all the pieces that were thought to be scared/dead tissue were gone from the spine and head. The only thing that remained was the mass in the back of the head which had not changed in size in three rounds of chemo. The neurologist was shocked by the results. I felt a level of comfort that there was no rush to decide to do either radiation beams or having surgery.

Sometimes when you do not get a response from God, you are to stand still. So right now, we are standing still and when God speaks, we will move. I truly understand why God said "fear not" first before saying stand still, because doing nothing is a scary thing. You wonder am I making the right decision. Say if we do not do the radiation beams will the cancer come back. Fear not Nicole...so I tell myself daily to stop second guessing our decision. I do not have the control; Phia is in God's hands, and He has been showing Himself mighty! Where she was...it is only God... where she is today!

CHAPTER 9
Resurgence

June 9, 2011

To God Be the Glory!
Sophia just received another victory this week; she turned 3 years old on Monday. When she was born, I did not realize the magnitude of the gift that God gave to us. I saw a baby girl and God saw a tool to reveal His Glory. We rejoiced all weekend and thanked God for His miraculous hand in this celebration. We celebrated Sophia's birthday on Saturday at the zoo and then an amusement park.

All the running she must have picked up a little germ. Sunday morning, she got sick and threw up and started freaking out. Sophia kept saying, "I don't want to be sick again." She seemed better and then when we were putting her to sleep that night she started screaming the same thing, "Aww, I don't want to be sick again" repeatedly. We were all freaked out. The thought of her getting sick again became a reality at that moment that not one of us wanted to deal with. Since she was diagnosed at 6 months this was the first time Sophia was able to articulate her feelings, which made all our hearts heavy. Dom had to sing to himself just to calm his nerves down.

June 12, 2011:
A MOTHER KNOWS

We had another sleepless night last night from Sophia crying, tossing, and turning. I have called the hospital several times this week and the same thing has been said each time, "Her symptoms don't sound like anything urgent, and I should keep monitoring her." Yesterday Phia did not want to eat and that is when my alarm bells started going off. Then last night in her tossing and turning, she cried out and said, "God help me." I called the hospital and talked to the fellow on call, and she was trying to make me feel like I was overreacting.

I said I do not call the hospital every time my daughter's nose runs; she has been fussing for a week now. I insisted on bringing her in. Sophia had a CAT Scan. While Juan was waiting with Phia to have X rays, the same doctor I spoke to this morning came to get me humbly to bring me back to the room. One of Sophia's primary team members was in the room with Juan. As soon as I saw his face and knew it was not a good report. He said something like a mother knows a child best and that her report was not good.

The CAT Scan showed a darken area on two spots of her brain. He felt that indicated that disease was present again. He recommended her to be admitted so she could have an MRI of the brain and total spine to get a better look at what is going on. So, we waited for hours to be admitted. My emotions were mixed. I did not know what to think or believe. I thought about a St. Jude Hospital commercial I saw the other night... The young girl's story drew me in. She had so much courage and remained positive through her adversity. I cried that night for her and her mom. They had to go back and continue to fight this horrible disease. Then the girl finally lost the battle.

My tears were flowing thinking about my own situation. The thought of coming out of this to be thrown back in was heart wrenching. Then to hear from our daughter's doctor the thing we feared the most was her scan. It was like time stood still. I could not believe this was real and at the same time I had a mixture of emotions going on. I felt confused. I felt angry. I felt like maybe they were looking at the wrong scans. I felt hopeful too. Hopeful because my mind could not comprehend that God would perform miracle after miracle on our daughter to leave us now. Please join us in prayer this time for a miraculous miracle right now. One without drugs, doctors, just the mighty hand of God at work on her behalf!

June 14, 2011

Waiting to take the MRI on Monday was rough because Sophia had to go to almost 1 pm without eating. This was extra difficult because the doctors put her on *steroids the night before, which spikes your appetite. The test took two hours because the head and total length of her spine was tested. The reports confirmed that cancer was back. Sophia's brain has a coating of cancer cells on the right side, a little on the left and the back. Her spine also shows a coating of disease present. I felt like the rug was pulled from underneath us once again. Just two ½ months ago Sophia's scans where clear.*

Everything within me thought this was behind us. I started the process to enroll her in a pre-school summer session that starts in July. We met with Make a Wish to plan a vacation, and now our reality is once again daily hospital visits. To make this process even harder, Sophia is old enough now to articulate her feelings which are heart wrenching. "Mommy I don't want to be sick," "Why did this happen," "I did not do anything," etc....

Knowing we were not going to start any kind of treatment that night we demanded to be discharged. Domonick's moving up ceremony from sixth grade was at 7pm and we did not want to disappoint him. Today Sophia's team met, and the recommendation is to do low dose radiation and 5 days of a chemo drug she has not used before but is very effective on this kind of cancer.

> At around 9 pm we re-admitted Sophia to the hospital to expedite the process for tomorrow morning. We do not have time on our side because today her pain level has increased rapidly, and her walking has become wobbly. That is a sign that the cancer is progressing quickly.

June 15, 2011
It is amazing how quick things can turn. Just a week ago we were celebrating Sophia's 3rd birthday. Today tears do not seem to stop falling as my heart grieves for my daughter's condition. One moment Sophia was laughing and running through our house and now she is lying in a hospital bed unable to move her legs. Last week there was so much joy in Phia's eyes and today all you see is suffering.

As we wait for an Anesthesiologist to start, while Phia is crying to eat, it pains us to not be able to relieve that discomfort. Sometimes life can be so cruel. Suffering is not a respecter of anyone. It creeps up on you when you least expectt it. This is when your faith is truly tried by the fire. My only comforting thought right now is in Psalm 112. In the New Living Translation it says, "When darkness overtakes the godly, light (His Light) will come bursting in." We sure could use a heavy dose of His light right now.

HOW MY FAITH BROUGHT ME THROUGH

June 16, 2011

We waited until 1:30 pm on Wednesday for the procedure room to get Sophia. She had a temporary line put back into her chest. Before they start external beam radiation treatment, the radiologist creates a treatment plan which involves positioning the body, making marks on the skin, and taking imaging scans. A mold like device is formed around the body to maintain the same position for the duration of treatments to the spine. Because Sophia will also need radiation to the head, a plastic mask was molded to her face. During treatment this is secured to the table, to hold the head in place. The molds are because the effectiveness of radiation treatment is hitting the attended site accurately. This took about an hour. Afterwards Sophia was able to recover from the anesthesia in her room. They have set her up with a pain pump. Because there's cancer compressing Sophia's spinal cord again, she lost complete movement in her legs. She is medicated heavenly because the swelling on the spinal cord is causing great pain. If you move Sophia just to change her, she is in agony. I had to tell myself this was not real, so I did not lose it. The process can take a week to start administering radiation. They were able to expedite the process for the spine and Sophia had her first treatment today. It takes a lot more time to plan for the head, so I was told she will not have treatment in that area until Monday or Tuesday. Sophia was in a lot of pain today. I asked them to up the medication levels. Phia slept most of the day due to the extreme medical treatments she underwent.

June 18, 2011

Sophia was brought down to radiation early Friday morning. Once she went into the room it only took about five minutes this time to administer the beams to her spine. It is amazing what you will allow to happen when it is a matter of life or death. People freak out at the thought of a *radiation leak and I am willing to allow my daughter to be exposed to it.*

Before they start the process, they close this huge door that is lined with lead and steel to keep those on the other side safe from radiation exposure. As my daughter is on the other side of this door, I have to tell myself this is a life saving measure as my heart is in disbelief. Within the five minutes I wait, I see nurses bringing other children from other radiation rooms out. As I see their scared faces, I try to shake off the saddest I was feeling.

My heart hurt for these kids and their families, and I felt a wave of discouragement that this was also my reality. When we returned to her room, Sophia still had a glazed-over look. This would last for anywhere from a few seconds to a minute. She had also been experiencing hand tremors for a few days now. I mentioned this to the team, and they ordered an EEG to motor the seizure activity. As the technician started attaching electrodes to Sophia's head, the fear of it induced a seizure. For the next few hours Sophia had multiple seizures. Sophia has been on seizure medication since last September. This was a strong indication that the disease in her brain had progressed.

Within this time Sophia's heart rate went extremely high and then her oxygen levels shot down. That with the combination of her being paralyzed again, severely constipated for a week, and now the seizures, I requested that they immediately move her to the POU (Pediatric Observation Unit) where they can better monitor her.

I was amazed that I was the one to requested that move and not the Fellow on the floor. But once again that was confirmation that I cannot slack for a minute being my daughter's advocate. After receiving meds, Sophia slept through the night.

June 21, 2011
Whose Report Will You Believe?

"I had fainted unless I had believed to see the goodness of the LORD in the land of the living. Wait on the LORD: be of good courage, and he shall strengthen thine heart: wait, I say, on the LORD." Psalm 27:13-14

I woke up around 2:30 am when I looked over at Sophia, she did not look right. She looked like she was having a seizure, so I frantically called the nurses. After they cleaned her up and the nurses felt she was stable they started to leave the room. I said she is still unresponsive; her eyes aren't opening. Within a few minutes Sophia's breathing was labored. The Fellow on call said they were going to have to put a breathing tube in. "Breathing tube, what do you mean?" I called Juan immediately and told him he had to get to the hospital quickly.

People started filling the room, lights started flashing, my head started spinning, and I felt like I could not breathe. What was going on? Code Blue was called at 3:15 am. Within a few minutes I was surrounded by strangers who were moving with a level of urgency. Some people were giving orders, while others were waiting for them. I felt all alone, there was not one friendly face. I could not believe that there was not one person in that room that knew Sophia.

Then a nurse that had previously taken care of Sophia came over. It was like God was saying I am here, I got you...you are not alone! Thank God, Juan got there right when they took Sophia for an x-ray. When we came back upstairs from the test, the Fellow asked to meet with us. She then proceeded to tell us that the disease has progressed, and the swelling has caused the brain to expand, which has pushed on the brain stem. She went onto to say that the damage was irreversible. The Fellow, the neurosurgeon, the head of Sophia's team all stressed that there was not anything else medically that the doctors could do.

The called for a transport team to move her to the Pediatric ICU at another Hospital. As they were getting Sophia ready for transport the ICU Fellow came up to us and asked us if we understood what was going on. I repeated to him what we were told. I went on to say that we are fully aware that from a professional position there is not anything else that could be done.

The ICU Fellow said angrily, "DO YOU REALIZE THAT YOUR DAUGHTER IS GOING TO DIE? She is going to be on life support and one of two things is going to happen. She is either going to slip away quietly or she is going to have to go through a bunch of procedures and then slip away. Do you want to really put all those assigned to her care through that?"

If God were going to send the Angel of Death, I believe in his Mercy He would have shielded us with love knowing this would be heartbreaking to say the least. I gained a confidence in the spirit knowing that the devil only comes at you like that when God is about to move! The devil cannot take your destiny, but he can beat you down so much that you give it up freely. The ICU Fellow was badgering us to pull the plug on our daughter before she even left the Cancer hospital.

I told him I am very aware of what is going on. We heard what the doctors had to say and now we are leaving room for God. I will not pull the plug on my daughter unless God says that to me. A few minutes later Juan pulled him aside and respectfully rebuked him for his actions. We also talked to his boss about his behavior and one of the doctors from the Cancer hospital called over to his boss as well.

Each hour of the remainder of the day felt like a week. After Sophia was settled at Pediatric ICU, we spoke to the doctor in charge who thank God was not a stranger to Sophia. She began to explain to us again Sophia's situation. She also went on to say that they would monitor her and assess her Brain Stem function. If the neurologist test showed no response to the assessment that the next step would be for a formal test by the ICU team and the neurologist team to be done to determine if Sophia is brain dead.

If Sophia failed that test, then six hours later they would do a second test to assess her. If she failed that test again then by law, Sophia would be declared brain dead, and the hospital would by law have the right to remove the life support. We could not believe what we were hearing. This was truly a horrible dream that we could not wake up from. The team came by to do the first assessment and the formal test was stopped because Sophia showed some response to the testing.

Hours later she did not show the same response, but it was not the formal test taken. When the neurologist said they would do the full test in the morning, I exhaled with relief. Psalm 30:5 jumped to my lips, "weeping may endure for a night, but joy cometh in the morning." The nurse moved Sophia with all the tubs, so I could sleep next to her. As I lied there the song that I kept singing all day came to my lips, "What I mighty God we serve. The Angels Bow before Him, Heaven, and Earthy Adore Him, what a mighty God we serve! My heart was heavy, but my spirit was light. Deep down, past the fear, past what I endured all day with my daughter, even past the tubes attached to her little body my soul trusted in God. An angelic presence came in as I was half asleep and I heard a small whisper say, it is going to be all right!

We need those who truly believe in the resurrection power of God to pray in absolute faith for God's Glory to be revealed through Sophia!

June 22, 2011
"Talitha cumi" meaning girl arise!!

HOW MY FAITH BROUGHT ME THROUGH

But as it is written, Eye hath not seen, nor ear heard, neither have entered into the heart of man, the things which God hath prepared for them that love him.
1 Corin: 2:9

I woke up today hoping that I saw an immediate manifestation from God. The monitors were the same, Sophia looked the same, and then the team came in to test Sophia. I started to become anxious, and I closed my eyes and prayed that God show me a sign of hope as I squeezed Juan's hand. The test started and when they got to the breath test and turned off the breathing machine, the Attending ICU Doctor said we must stop the test to determine brain death because Sophia is making breath on her own!

The team seemed shocked, while Juan and my heart rejoiced in those few words. The ICU doctor came by later in the day by herself and performed the breathing test again and it showed the same result! This by doctor's standards was not supposed to happen today! I rejoice over this milestone blessing knowing that God's power is perfected in our weakness!

As we prayed tonight, Sophia's breath was going past the machine setting as we called on the Throne Room. Her lungs were making full breaths on her own! God is

Able!!! We need those who truly believe in the resurrection power of God to pray in absolute faith for God to reveal His Glory through Sophia's complete healing. That she would go on to testify to what He did for her!

I did not write a journal entry the day Sophia passed away; because it felt like time stood still. On the morning of June 23rd, I recall waking up with an immense feeling of joy in my heart. It was a profound celebratory feeling unlike anything I had experienced before.

For the first time since God had forewarned me of my daughter's suffering, I felt a deep knowing within me that she would be healed. It was not merely a feeling of hope or belief; it was a certainty deep within my spirit. I could not help but sing as I got dressed and drove to the hospital. I wish I could recall the gospel song I sang; its melody filled me with a sense of anticipation and expectation.

Navigating the hospital halls, I felt like I was skipping with excitement. In the waiting room, a few members from my church offered words of comfort, speaking of God's healing power in Sophia's situation. Their words resonated with me, strengthening my confidence that this day would mark a turnaround in her condition.

However, upon stepping into her room and laying eyes on her, I knew immediately she was gone. Her presence was no longer there, even as her body continued to breathe through the machine. I stood there for what felt like an eternity, though it was only a few minutes.

Juan's head was down when I asked him when the angel came for her, he recounted hearing God's voice saying it was time to let her go. He felt the presence of the death angel at three in the morning, and then Sophia's spirit departed. As I reached for her hand, the warmth I once felt was gone, replaced by a chilling emptiness.

Juan, Dom, and our friends and family in the waiting room all took turns saying goodbye. I held onto Sophia until the doctors arrived to perform the last and final test, unable to let go until the very end.

June 24, 2011
Time to Go Home June (6-6-08 to 6-23-11)

Sophia Nicole Roman fought the good fight of faith. God know in his infinite mercy it was Sophia's time to go home and she was ready. The first Christian song our daughter started singing was "I will Rise." I loved the song but when she sang the chorus "I will rise when He calls my name, no more sorrow, no more pain" I cried because I felt like she was singing it as a forthcoming declaration.

She knew He was going to call her name soon! She did not sing the song with the innocence of a two-year-old; she sang it from the place of someone who has gone through something and was ready to go when God was ready to take her. Several weeks ago, Sophia started saying, "Mommy I want to go home." I would tell her she was home. I thought she was saying it because we moved a few months ago. Then a week before she got sick, when she stated she wanted to go home, I asked her "what home are you talking about? Are you talking home with Father God where Grandpa Tom is?" She never answered me but the look she gave spoke to my heart. The look said, mommy I am sad because I do not want to leave you but I am tired. I said please do not leave mommy, and I hugged her. I felt weighed by guilt because my baby held on in the ICU because of my pleas.

God called Sophia's name and she rose at 7:23 pm yesterday. The angels were having a party in heaven for her spirit making the journey back home! RIP my beloved daughter our lives will be forever changed by your imprint on our hearts.

HOW MY FAITH BROUGHT ME THROUGH

~~~

As we reflect on the heavy content we just read, I want to assure you that my intention is not to leave you in despair. Let us continue this journey together, knowing that as we navigate through the sorrow, we will find hope and restoration in the comforting presence of God. Before we continue, let us pray:

Father God,

We come before you with heavy hearts, mindful of those who have just finished reading about the suffering and death of a child. I recognize the profound weight and sorrow that such words can carry, and I lift those who are grappling with these emotions.

Lord, I pray for your comforting presence to wrap around each reader who has been touched by this story. I ask for your grace to release any heaviness they may be feeling, and for your healing touch to mend the wounds of loss that they may have suffered and still be carrying.

May they find comfort in knowing that you were ever-present throughout the journey of Sophia's life, and that your love never wavered, even in the midst of suffering. Grant them the strength to see beyond the pain and to find healing, hope and restoration through You.

NICOLE ESTELLE ROMAN

Help them to hold onto the memories of love and joy shared with their precious loved one's who are no longer with them, and to find peace in the knowledge that they are now cradled in Your loving arms.

In the name of Jesus Christ, our ultimate source of comfort and hope, we pray,

Amen.

CHAPTER 10
Goodbye

After we left the hospital without our baby, Juan, Dom, and I all felt shell-shocked and lost. The silence in the car on the way home seemed to amplify the emptiness within us, drowning out even the sound of our breaths. The weight of our loss pressed down on us like a suffocating force.

My mind flooded with anguish and unanswered questions. Thoughts of my baby lying alone on a cold slab, the fate of her tiny body, the haunting memory of her last breath – this tormented me relentlessly. I constantly prayed for God's peace to calm and overtake me.

The days following her passing were a blur. The grief engulfed us like a tidal wave, leaving us drowning in a sea of tears and despair. Once filled with laughter and cherished memories of our beloved Sophia, our home now ached from her absence. Each room seemed haunted by Sophia's memory, a painful reminder of the joy we had lost.

Having experienced a lot of grief before, I thought I understood its depths. But nothing could have prepared me for the unbearable pain of losing a child. I found myself silently praying for the pain to end, for my heart to stop beating beneath the weight of such unbearable sorrow.

As we approached Sophia's funeral, time seemed to stand still, the world frozen in a moment of unbearable grief. Numbness crept over us like a dense fog, shielding us from the full force of our emotions as we moved through the day in a daze. Despite our attempts to find comfort, we each retreated into our sunken place, grappling with the overwhelming darkness that threatened to consume us.

As we planned for her funeral, the harsh reality of our loss began to sink in, serving as a stark reminder that life would never be the same. The burden of grief weighed heavily on me, pressing down like an unbearable load, rendering even the simplest tasks unbearable. Each moment dragged on, filled with an overwhelming desire to escape the agony.

HOW MY FAITH BROUGHT ME THROUGH

I reached out to my doctor for assistance. Despite my deep faith in God's healing power, I recognized the need for additional and immediate support to help me through the crushing pain. Seeking help was not a sign of weakness or lack of faith. Instead, it was an act of love toward myself by acknowledging my limitations and being proactive to help me grieve forward. Even as a woman of faith, I understood that sometimes divine intervention works hand in hand with earthly assistance to provide what is needed to help someone from drowning in despair.

Amidst the darkness, there were flickers of light. Friends and family rallied around us shortly after Sophia passed. They were offering their support and assistance in our time of need. Their acts of kindness, no matter how small, were beacons of hope in our darkest hours. I remember how the phone was ringing non-stop. People asked if I needed anything or what they should bring to the repass. My cousin Jeanna and my friend Danielle indeed came to my rescue. They saw I needed to be in a place to make decisions. Instead of asking what we needed, they showed up and filled the gaps, easing our burden in any way they could. Whether it was cleaning our home, organizing the funeral arrangements, or simply being a shoulder to lean on, their presence was a lifeline in our time of need.

Looking back, I now realize that genuine compassion is expressed through actions. It is about seeing the need and stepping in to fulfill it, whether small or insignificant. In our darkest hour, the love in action truly ministered to our souls, helping lift the burden while we grieved forward. When someone is suffering, they may not even know what they need, let alone have the capacity to articulate it.

Even if not in autopilot mode, the griever may not want to impose on others by asking for help. That is why it is so important for friends and family to step in and offer support without waiting to be asked. Observing and sensing their needs, whether practical assistance like cleaning or cooking, or offering emotional support through a simple act of one's presence, can provide comfort during someone's darkest days. The smallest gestures can make the most significant difference in someone's healing journey.

Sophia's wake passed by in a blur. During the private viewing, I could not help but notice how she looked like a beautiful angel, serene and peaceful. We decided to have a closed casket, knowing that it would be too difficult for many to see s child lying there.

HOW MY FAITH BROUGHT ME THROUGH

Her funeral took place at the church where I had grown up, thanks to the kindness of Reverend Thomas Johnson from Mount Bethel Baptist Church. I will always be grateful for his compassion and kindness during our time of need. The church opened its doors to us, offering comfort and support, for which I am forever grateful.

As I sat through the service, the psalmist's voice filled the air, and something stirred within me. Despite the overwhelming grief, my spirit could not help but leap to my feet with joy. At that moment, I realized Sophia had made it home, safe in the arms of our Father. I danced joyfully for Phia, finishing her race strong and her newfound peace. Our suffering with Sophia was the cost of the oil in our lives, as I praised God for his little warrior who now gets to rest.

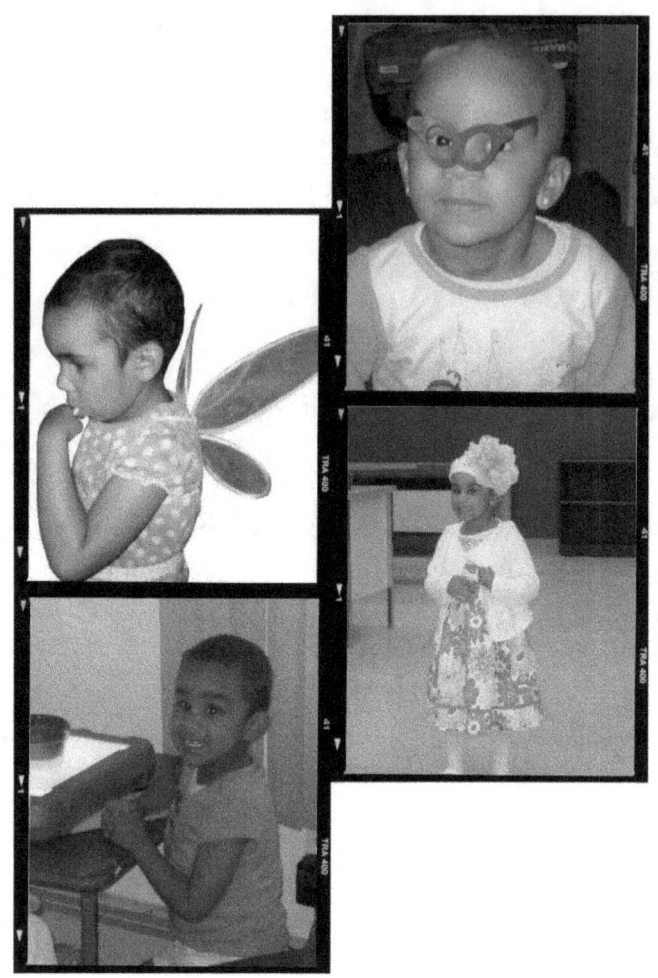

HOW MY FAITH BROUGHT ME THROUGH

NICOLE ESTELLE ROMAN

CHAPTER 11
After The Ground Settles

Shortly after the funeral, our son spent time with Grandma for the month. We made a choice, recognizing that neither Juan nor I could provide him with the support he needed in our state of devastation. My mother and Dom coped similarly, finding comfort in activities, so I hoped this would benefit them. Or at least, I prayed it would.

Reflecting on that choice we made, I realize now that pain and suffering can lead to selfishness, as it becomes solely about survival. Just as in the airplane safety protocol, where you must secure your oxygen mask before assisting others, we decided to send Dom to my mother's so we could guarantee our oxygen. It felt both selfish and unselfish simultaneously. I could not bear the thought of neglecting my son, especially when I knew I lacked the capacity and will to continue after Sophia's passing. He deserved someone who could be fully present and supportive as he grappled with the loss of his sister. My mother was the better choice to help our son at that moment.

When I informed Dom that he would spend a month at Grandma's, I explained to him the necessity of the situation. I needed time to gather myself and become better equipped to support him. I told him, "I do not want to be one of those parents lost in their pain," I emphasized, "neglecting the child who still needs them." I pleaded with him to understand and grant me this month to heal, while he and Grandma created new memories together.

Juan and I decided to escape for a week, feeling suffocated by the weight of our emotions. We needed distance from the house, the painful reminders, and the overwhelming sorrow. However, we soon discovered that no matter how far we traveled, the pain followed. Upon returning home, I found myself retreating into a dark room, seeking refuge under covers, hoping to sleep away from the anguish. But there was no relief. When I was awake, I would ache to hold Sophia, and I kept asking God to let me come home.

HOW MY FAITH BROUGHT ME THROUGH

July 6, 2011

A week ago, we buried our daughter, and tomorrow marks two weeks since we held Phia and said goodbye.

The Bible says you must have childlike faith to enter the Kingdom of God. I utterly understood that when we came to the end of this journey with Sophia. Despite the doctor's reports, we believed God had the last say. We thought that if it were God's will for her to live, Sophia would, which would defy all-natural law.

My pride has been screaming, "You are a fool for telling everyone that God was going to heal Sophia even when her brain stem suffered irreversible damage." Then the spirit within me says, "Isn't that childlike faith?" Faith believes God can do it even if He chooses not to. Faith trusts that God knows the best course in His infinite wisdom.

In the wake, someone I did not know came up to me to offer their condolences. The woman asked me if I would still write on Sophia's blog. I thought that was a strange thing to say. I started this journal to update family and friends on Sophia's progress and to give Sophia a record of what God brought her through when she got older. Then, as the week unfolded, I realized that this journal had become part of my life. In some way, it touched the lives of those who read it. I was hesitating to write on the website after the cancer spread the first time. My pride was saying, "You are a fool to be so transparent; say if she dies, your pain will be on public display."

Then I thought about how only being truthful and transparent ministers to me. I did not want Sophia or my family to go through this for naught. That woman at the wake was confirmation that this was not in vain. We will never know how far-reaching Sophia's ministry indeed was. But I am thankful that Juan and I were obedient to aid in her ministry. We never held her testimonies of victories, nor did we downplay her defeats. In three short years, Sophia taught those watching what faith is.

Sophia praised God despite her current situation and reminded those around her to pray. Her faith indeed became her eyes. We loved our little girl with everything within us and tried our best to show her that. We know our daughter is in a better place. We did not want Sophia to suffer anymore, nor keep her from going home when God called. Our spirit knows Sophia fulfilled her assignment, but as parents, our hearts broke. The day she died, all our hopes and dreams for her died with her. Our family vision changed forever, and now we must figure out how to move forward without her, and not allow the grief to overshadow us from raising our son. Grief is not a day-by-day thing; it is a moment-by-moment process. One moment, we can be okay, and the next, the sadness hits us like a slag hammer. I pray that no one reading this has to ever walk in our shoes. Love your children with everything you have. Love those God places around you, and do not put off tomorrow what you can do today!

We are forever grateful for all the support and love shown to us. Because of the generosity that has outpoured on us, we were able to give our baby a proper Homegoing. Thank you all for being a blessing. I pray God outpours blessings upon you and your household for being so kind to one of His!

That is what we put on the back of the prayer card:

<u>Going Home</u>
"I want to go home," you often said.
We assumed you meant an "earthly" place.
But now, we know, Sophia, you meant with God instead.
He saw you getting tired of the fight; a cure was not to be.
So, He wrapped you in His loving arms and whispered, "Come with Me."
You carried your cross with courage until the end
With tears, we watched you slip away.
Our hearts are breaking as we pray for you to stay.

But when we saw you were sleeping,
So peaceful and free from pain.
How could we wish to hold you back?
It broke our hearts to lose our baby girl.
But know, you did not go alone.
Part of us went with you,
the day God took you home.
Love,
Mommy, Daddy, and Dommy

My heart broke; it was crushed to pieces, swirling like the things caught up in a destructive tornado. The weight of grief made it hard to breathe as if I had developed asthma. I confided in Juan, and he admitted to the same struggle to breathe. As the grief deepened, depression gripped me, leaving me exhausted constantly. It took every ounce of strength to muster the will to get out of bed each day.

Besides wrestling with the emptiness in my heart from the loss of my baby, I struggled with extreme loneliness as I tried to make sense of something so utterly senseless. The journey felt especially isolated during Sophia's illness because most people did not know how to confront the reality of a sick child. But the loneliness intensified after her passing.

HOW MY FAITH BROUGHT ME THROUGH

The silence was deafening; the phone hardly rang. People did not know what to say. When they did call, it seemed they were tiptoeing around the subject, avoiding mentioning her name. I wanted to cry out to tell them it was okay to say her name; avoiding it made me feel worse.

Even though Sophia is no longer here with us, she will always be my daughter, and I will always want to talk about her. Death does not diminish the longing, love, or desire to keep her memory alive. True comfort comes from those who show gentleness, kindness, and willingness to listen.

Our lives became the nightmare that most parents fear. We unwillingly became members of a club no one wishes to join: "Parents who have lost a child." It defies the natural order, where children are supposed to outlive their parents. My mother buried my sister at forty-five, and now I buried my daughter at three years old. I never wanted to join this club, and my prayers are that no one else in my family would ever experience this type of pain. I would not even wish this on my worst enemy; this is a pain no one should ever endure.

A month after Sophia transitioned, someone said to me, "Sophia cannot rest because you're not okay." Those words shook my heart. The thought of my baby going through all the hell she endured on this earth, not to rest in her eternal resting place, pained me deeply. I do not believe in communicating with spirits, except for the Holy Spirit. But I needed to hear those words. It was a jolt I needed. I understood that remaining in this state of despair was not a fitting tribute to Sophia's memory.

When it was time to pick up Dom from my mother's house, I spent a few days there. During that time, we decided to visit a small water park on a military base. While we were there, Dom asked me to join him on the tube slide. Initially, I hesitated, but then I thought I must live for Sophia's sake, as she will never experience such simple pleasures. I would not say I liked the confining feeling of being in an enclosed hot tube shooting through the dark waters.

Despite my discomfort with the confined space and the rush of water in the dark, hot tube, I summoned the courage to go down the slide with Dom. It seemed like a reflection of my struggles, of feeling trapped in a dark, hot situation. However, as we emerged into the brightness and hit the water below, a realization dawned on me: I needed to make a conscious choice to live, not just for myself, or because Sophia could not, but for my son. He was the life

HOW MY FAITH BROUGHT ME THROUGH

preserver God brought into my life that I need to keep me afloat.

When I heard God tell me I would raise Dom as my son, I believed I would be the one God used to save him. Little did I know he would end up saving me. His presence in my life became my lifeline, a reason to get up every day, and a testament to the unexpected ways in which love can stabilize you, even in turbulent times.

As the light tried to break it, I began to despise how I felt, knowing deep down I could not continue like this. The urgent need consumed me to heal by any means necessary. When I found the strength to pray, I cried out for help. In moments when I could not even lift my head, I prayed in tongues, with the Holy Spirit communicating to God on my behalf. I allowed myself to cry when my heart ached. The times when I stayed in bed, unwilling to face the world, were decreasing. I delved into one grief book after another, sought comfort in conversations with fellow parents who had lost children, and actively searched for a Christian therapist.

I found a peer-facilitated grief group for parents who had lost a child. However, someone I knew well advised me against it, expressing concern that I might focus on ministering to others' hearts and neglecting my own.

Despite considering their words, I was desperate to find something to ease the pain. Moreover, Juan and I felt we could benefit from the support of those who had navigated through similar dark waters.

On the day we attended the group, I felt hopeful, believing it would be a positive step forward for Juan and me. However, everyone who spoke introduced themselves as their dead child's name. I was troubled by how their identities seemed to become the child they lost. During the sharing time, parents expressed their pain over losing their children, some of whom passed 10, 15, and 30 years ago. The way they poured out the pain felt like their child had just passed, and Juan and I were the ones wet behind our ears being there a month after our loss. The room felt like a pot full of simmering pain, waiting for someone to stir it for it to bubble over.

As the person had warned, I tried to minister to their pain. Juan whispered to me, "I have to leave; they are making me feel like killing myself." We had expected to receive coping techniques, encouragement, and reassurance that things would get better. Instead, we left feeling worse than when we arrived. They did not offer any hope, which was what we desperately needed.

HOW MY FAITH BROUGHT ME THROUGH

A few days later, a co-worker called to check on me. She shared how her son shot and killed himself by playing a gun game with his friends. During our conversation, she said, "Now you can't leave the Tri-State area." Being perplexed. I asked her why you would say that. She responded, "Because you buried your daughter here." She said, "Now you are tied to the area." Then she said, "My son passed away nine years ago." She felt like she owed it to him to continue visiting him at the cemetery.

My co-worker's conversation and the insights shared by participants in the grief group opened my eyes to a profound truth that propelled me forward in my healing journey. I realized that fear and guilt can become barriers to true healing.

The fear of letting go of grief stems from the misconception that by releasing our grief, we are letting go of our loved ones. In holding onto grief, we mistakenly believe we are holding onto a connection with the person we lost. However, it is essential to understand that our love for them transcends grief, and they will always have a special place in our hearts, notwithstanding our grief.

Moreover, some people feel guilty about allowing their hearts to heal, because they perceive it as a reflection of their love for the departed. They question themselves, wondering how to be happy, smile, or have fun while their loved ones cannot. This guilt can hinder the healing process, as it falsely equates healing with a lack of love or respect for the deceased.

Embracing healing and finding joy in life honors the memory of our loved ones. It acknowledges that they would want us to live fully and cherish the moments we have. Walking towards healing does not diminish our love for them; instead, it signifies our ability to carry their love with us as we continue our journey.

As I tried to heal forward, the "why" question echoed relentlessly in my heart. I could not fathom the reason why our family endured such pain. I know her life had ministered to countless people. I witnessed hearts turning back to God, family members rediscovering their faith, and numerous souls touched by Sophia's resilience, yet I could not reconcile the why in my heart.

January 16, 2012

Finding myself at a crossroads of grief and purpose, I stumbled upon The American Childhood Cancer Organization in my search for meaning. As I read about the organization, I could not help but reflect on how their support could have eased our own family's struggles during

HOW MY FAITH BROUGHT ME THROUGH

Sophia's battle with cancer. It was as if a beacon of hope had illuminated my path forward, urging me to reach out and offer my assistance.

Within a month, the organization appointed me a board member. Drawing upon my background in marketing, I immediately recognized the opportunity to leverage my skills and expertise to amplify awareness of childhood cancer and the urgent need for funding and research.

Around the same time, we welcomed a yellow lab rescue puppy into our home. We named him "Barney," in honor of Sophia's favorite show, as a tribute to the joy it brought her. We hoped Barney could help fill the void we were feeling and get some much-needed pleasure back into our household.

I constantly fought to regain a sense of normalcy and make sense of everything we went through. Desperate to escape the pain, I attempted to rush through the grieving process, hoping to find relief quickly. The thought of living with this profound emptiness in my heart for the rest of my days was unfathomable, driving me to find something to ease the pain like a quick fix.

Yet, I soon discovered that grief cannot be rushed or swept aside by busyness. In this journey through grief, I realized that healing takes time, patience, and acceptance. It cannot be rushed or forced; it must be expressed. And though the road may be long and arduous, I began to understand that true healing comes when you allow yourself to feel it thoroughly and give voice to what you feel. Grief does not want to let you go, so you must be intentional to heal forward.

HOW MY FAITH BROUGHT ME THROUGH

HOW MY FAITH BROUGHT ME THROUGH

CHAPTER 12
Therapy's Impact

Being intentional in your healing journey begins with a deep desire for healing. It is a conscious choice that you must actively pursue because grief has a way of holding onto your heart tightly. Deciding to choose life over mere existence is paramount. You have to firmly resolve in your mind that you are opting for active participation in moving forward toward healing.

Prayer is a powerful tool in this process, but it is essential to recognize that if you are not open to healing, it is as if you are tying the hands of any divine intervention. Through my years of serving in a church, I have witnessed firsthand that deliverance or healing often does not manifest until a person's heart is genuinely receptive to it. This openness, this willingness to confront your pain and actively seek healing, ultimately unlocks the path to profound transformation and restoration. We must give God something to work with.

I was genuinely open to healing because I did not know how to function under the weight of grief. Then, an answered prayer came knocking at my door, literally. A counselor from a wonderful organization in New Jersey called the Emmanuel Cancer Foundation came once a month to check on me. After Sophia passed, the counselor came by and informed me that she was leaving to work at the Gilda Radner's Cancer Foundation. She mentioned they were about to start a six-week bereavement course that she thought I would benefit from. Initially hesitant, I shared with her that I had tried a group setting before, and it did not turn out well. Nevertheless, she assured me that this course was different; there was only one other woman in it, and they followed a structured agenda.

Little did I know at that moment that this decision was instrumental to my healing journey. Being able to give voice to my pain within this structured setting was when true healing began for me. Therapy is not just about acknowledging the hurt that we carry within; it is about actively engaging with it, allowing ourselves to feel and express what lies under the surface. I held onto my pain, burying it deep within, thinking that what I saw my baby endured was too difficult for others to bear. But I needed to release it because unexpressed pain does not vanish. It only festers and grows, consuming us from within.

Talking with the two women who were not part of my life created a safe environment for me to share. I did not want to burden anyone's heart with the horror of the cancer wreckage I witnessed. When I finally felt safe to share the pain I was carrying, to give it a voice, I experienced a transformative shift. Verbalizing my emotions allowed me to confront the ugliness head-on and free myself in a way I never could before. Sharing my pain with those who understood and empathized with me brought a sense of validation and belonging I had long been missing. No longer did I feel alone in my struggles; instead, I found comfort in the shared understanding of others who had walked a similar path. Through giving voice to my pain, I began to unravel the complexities of my grief, slowly but surely finding my feeling a little lighter, a little more at peace.

As I delved deeper into therapy, unpacking my thoughts, fears, traumas, and pain, I found myself naturally bringing these revelations into prayer. Therapy served as the switch that illuminated the darkness within me, allowing God to minister to my heart in ways I could not have imagined. Each session became a safe place where I could lay down my burdens and invite divine intervention into my healing journey. Through prayer, I sought comfort, clarity, and strength while trusting in God's guidance as He began to put the pieces back into my heart. Engaging in therapy allowed me to approach my healing journey with intentionality, while my faith brought me before the ultimate Healer.

CHAPTER 13
God's Time

As I chose to live each day, I often heard, "Time heals all wounds." While I acknowledge that with time, wounds can gradually mend, I have come to understand firsthand that true healing stems not from the passage of time but from the boundless love of a compassionate Father, who serves as the ultimate healer. Through the significant losses I have experienced in my life, I have witnessed the gentle hand of God piecing together the fragments of my heart with grace and tenderness.

Healing, I have come to realize, is a journey—a process marked by moments of progress and setbacks. For a long time, there were times when I felt like I had made significant strides, only to be unexpectedly thrown into a whirlwind of emotions by a triggering memory. Yet, just like a wound on the arm, healing unfolds gradually. Initially, it may appear raw and tender, but with each passing day, it begins to show signs of improvement until, eventually, a scab forms and true healing emerges.

The ultimate lesson lies in the process of walking forward through the grief, embracing a slow dance of living moment by moment, then day by day, until the heart graciously allows the gift of release. God, in His infinite grace, uses time as a tool to minister to our wounded hearts, delicately putting the shattered pieces back together.

With each passing moment, the sharp sting of pain gradually fades away, creating space for acceptance and the slow, steady onset of healing to take root. Though the path to healing may twist and turn, marked by unpredictable ups and downs, time offers us the chance to grow and evolve. From the depths of despair, we emerge with newfound wisdom and perspective, transformed by the journey of grief and loss. Time becomes more than just a measure of the moments we've lost—it becomes a testament to our resilience, our capacity for hope, and the enduring strength of the human spirit to rise above even the most profound heartache.

HOW MY FAITH BROUGHT ME THROUGH

It took me years to realize that my healing journey was incomplete. I had thought I had dealt with everything, but over time, God revealed to me that there were layers to healing. Then, He revealed one thing I had been holding onto—an emotion that had been hindering my progress toward complete healing. Suddenly, like a bolt of lightning, it became clear: I harbored anger. Anger directed at God for all the suffering I had endured. It was not just the pain of watching Sophia suffer and pass away but also grappling with a miscarriage, financial ruin, marital issues, further losses of family members, and struggles with my health. I felt cheated out of my fairytale, and I questioned whether God loved me.

As these emotions surfaced, I could not hold back the tears. For so long, I had buried my disappointment, bitterness, and anger, unknowingly allowing them to decay my joy, peace, and relationship with God. The anger kept me stuck on autopilot, unable to fully engage with life. But the moment I let go of anger, an immediate weight lifted off my shoulders and my heart. It was as if a fog had lifted, and suddenly, I could see and hear God again.

When I finally released the grip of anger, I opened myself up to God's healing touch in a way I had not allowed myself to experience in years. It was as if a floodgate had opened, and His love poured into every crevice of my wounded heart. With the weight of resentment lifted, I found myself liberated to move forward in every aspect of my life. My false perceptions began to crumble, and I could again perceive the overwhelming love of God with clarity that my bitterness had overshadowed. It was a profound transformation—a reawakening of the truth of who God truly is.

Left unchecked and allowed to fester, anger can quickly become a toxic poison that impedes our ability to move forward and heal. Like a destructive force, it eats away at our peace of mind, clouding our judgment and distorting our perceptions. When we hold onto anger, we imprison ourselves in a cycle of bitterness and resentment, trapping us in a state of emotional paralysis.

Instead of moving forward in our healing journey, we find ourselves stuck in a chaos of negativity, unable to break free from the shackles of our own making. Anger closes our eyes to the possibility of forgiveness, reconciliation, and growth, keeping us chained to the past and hindering our ability to embrace the present moment. To move forward and experience true healing, we must confront and release the toxic grip of anger, allowing grace, compassion, and renewal to enter our hearts.

HOW MY FAITH BROUGHT ME THROUGH

Over time, we unearth profound lessons that resonate deep within our souls in the container of grief. Through the veil of tears and the ache of loss, we discover the resilience of the human spirit, with God giving us the strength to endure unimaginable pain and emerge stronger on the other side.

Grief teaches us the fleeting nature of life, urging us to cherish each moment and hold dear to the ones we love. It reminds us of the interconnectedness of all beings, inviting us to extend empathy and kindness to ourselves and others as we navigate the rocky terrain of loss. Grief unveils the transformative power of vulnerability, inviting us to lean into our pain and find comfort in the shared experience of our humanity.

Through the veil of tears and the ache of loss, we discover the resilience of the human spirit over time, with God giving us the strength to endure unimaginable pain and emerge stronger on the other side. My faith brought me through the darkest of times, guiding me along a path illuminated by the unwavering presence and boundless love of God.

In moments of despair and sorrow, He sent comfort as His love carried me through. Through my relationship with Him, I was strengthened to face each day, knowing He is my constant source of strength and guidance, leading me through every challenge with unwavering love. In His light, I discovered the power of releasing the pain, anger, and grief to fully walk in the beauty of restoration, and the hope and promise of a brighter tomorrow.

CHAPTER 14
Beauty from Ashes

June 20, 2012

Beauty from Ashes!

To appoint unto them that mourn in Zion, to give them beauty for ashes, the oil of joy for mourning, the garment of praise for the spirit of heaviness; that they might be called trees of righteousness, the planting of the Lord, that he might be glorified.
Isaiah 61:3

November 5, 2011: Sophia's vision therapist texted me about a dream she had. She was coming over to my house for a session, and Sophia answered the door. Sophia looked healthy, happy, and said, "Ms. Maria, Mommy is having a baby!" After reading the text, I took a home pregnancy test an hour later. It took me a good hour to look at the results because I was emotional. The stick read positive.

I burst into tears because fear instantly gripped my heart. I cried out to God, saying I cannot endure this again. My heart was so heavy dealing with the grief of losing Phia; how could I go through 9 months of pregnancy? After pulling myself together, I walked to my doctor to take another pregnancy test to make sure before telling Juan.

Juan had the same reaction as I did. A week later, we had an ultrasound scheduled to determine how far along I was. I thought I could not be more than a few weeks. Surprisingly, I was about nine weeks into the pregnancy, which moved my due date to June. At that moment, I truly realized that this baby was a gift from God.

June was the month Sophia was born, and the same month she passed, God was blessing us in the place of our most incredible suffering! We hoped the baby would come early to help us deal with Sophia's birthday on the sixth. As the days rolled by, I could not understand why God did not honor my request. Then this morning, as the contractions got worse and we made our way to the hospital, it dawned on me that today, the season changed from spring to summer!

The realization had my spirit leap; today, it signified a change of seasons for my family. We went from

HOW MY FAITH BROUGHT ME THROUGH

a season of sorrow and mourning to one of Joy! At 4:19 pm, I gave birth to our daughter, Isabella Joy Roman. She weighed 9.2 pounds and was twenty-one inches long! I thank God for knowing what we needed more than we did! My heart is filled with gratitude that God even used Sophia in a dream to let us know about what He was about to bless us with. This Saturday marks a year that Sophia went home to be with God. We miss her more than words can truly express, but we are thankful God is a restorer, and His word does not lie. Today, we saw beauty rise from our ashes!

~~~~~

As I reflect on that journal entry, my mind drifts back to that sweet memory when Juan and I shared as we prayed over what to name our unborn daughter. The memory is vivid: as we went before God, the anticipation of getting guidance. I remember as I voiced my love for the name Isabella, drawn to its profound meaning—a devotion to God, a symbol of His oath. As we prayed, we heard God's gentle whisper confirming the name Isabella and the revelation of adding Joy because of His promise of restored joy. And indeed, true to His word, Isabella Joy has become a beacon of joy and restoration in our lives, a true blessing from our loving Father.

It is truly remarkable to emerge from darkness into the warmth of joy and love. In this season of my life, the thought overwhelms me, "Oh, how He loves me!" The depth of this love envelops me, reminding me that the Father cherishes me. It is a gift beyond measure, sparking unending praise and gratitude within my heart.

Isabella Sleeping Beauty

Tummy Time!

CHAPTER 15
Hope Lives

"Hope deferred makes the heart sick, but a longing fulfilled is a tree of life."
Proverbs 13:12 (NIV)

In the depths of despair, we faced the unimaginable:
- The diagnosis of our daughter's illness.
- The grueling journey of treatment.
- The devastating loss that shattered our world.

Yet, amid the darkness, the light of our faith illuminated every step we took forward.

In our darkest hours, our faith propelled us through fear, suffering, death, and healing. Though crushed by grief and uncertainty, God's love gently pieced together the fragments of our shattered hearts. I am grateful we did not give up along the way because we would never have tasted the sweetness of restoration.

Through prayer and perseverance, I discovered the transformative power of healing. It was not a quick fix or an easy road but a journey of resilience and renewal. With each passing day, I invested time and energy into my healing process, confronting the pain and embracing the possibility of being made whole.

As I walked this healing path, I lived intentionally, embracing each moment with gratitude and purpose. Though the scars of our journey remain, they testify to our strength and resilience.

Today, I stand on the other side of darkness, not unscathed but stronger and more steadfast in my faith. I have witnessed the miraculous power of love and redemption and I am grateful for the blessings that my faith brought me through!

Thirteen years have passed since I held my daughter Sophia. We lived so much life in those years. Today, hope and joy have replaced pain and suffering. I now share my daughter's life and struggles to help others navigate through the depths of despair that loss brings.

Holidays, once filled with sorrow, now bear the warmth of cherished memories of our beloved Sophia and new memories made with our family. Gratitude floods my soul as I reflect on the choice to persevere, the resilience granted by divine grace. God did not allow me to quit, so I am profoundly thankful as I embrace the calm after the storm.

Walking alongside Sophia through her journey gifted me with countless blessings. This little angel taught me the invaluable lessons of living in the present, savoring each moment, and loving without constraints. Because of Sophia, I have become a more nurturing mother to Dom and Bella. Caring for her throughout her trial has molded me into a more empathetic and compassionate servant.

May these words echo within your soul, leading you through the darkest nights and lighting the way to a brighter tomorrow. Embrace each dawn with unwavering determination, for within the broken pieces of grief lie the seeds of restoration. Allow God to water these seeds; beauty will bloom again as seasons change. Take comfort in knowing that despite life's trials, there is limitless potential for hope, love, and purpose to thrive within your heart again, for nothing is too complicated for God! I speak to the faintheart, "Faith be ignited," so you can testify how your faith brought you through!

NICOLE ESTELLE ROMAN

Juan, Nicole, Dom, & Bella

HOW MY FAITH BROUGHT ME THROUGH

HOW MY FAITH BROUGHT ME THROUGH

CHAPTER 16
The Gift of Prayer

I can testify that the prayers that besieged heaven on our behalf are what sustained us. I have no doubt that the prayers of the righteous played a vital role at every twist and turn of our journey. Whether they came from leaders, family, friends, or even strangers whose paths crossed ours, their intercession acted as a spiritual defibrillator, sending revitalizing shock waves when we felt like we were flatlining.

Each prayer, whispered with sincerity and love, brought light forth in our darkest hours, illuminating our path and reminding us of the boundless power of God's divine grace. Prayer proved to be one of the most profound blessings we received, a lifeline that kept us from giving up.

May these prayer's serve as a source of comfort and inspiration on your own journey to healing. From my heart to yours, may you find strength and comfort as you approach the throne of grace.

Prayer of Healing
Almighty God,

We come before you, lifting those battling illness and struggling with their health. You are the Divine Physician, the source of healing and comfort. We ask for your healing touch to rest upon those who need it. Bring restoration to their bodies, minds, and spirits.

Scripture assures us in James 5:14-15: "Is anyone among you sick? Let them call the elders of the church to pray for them and anoint them with oil in the name of the Lord. And the prayer offered in faith will make the sick person well; the Lord will raise them up. If they have sinned, they will be forgiven."

We trust in your promise of healing, knowing that You are always faithful to your Word. Help us accept how you chose to heal them. May those suffering find comfort in your presence and strength in their weakness. Grant them the peace that surpasses all understanding, knowing that You will never leave or forsake them.

Lord, we thank you for your agape love and compassion towards us. May your healing power flow through every part of their being, bringing wholeness and renewal. Grant them the courage and perseverance to face each day with hope and trust in your divine plan.

In Jesus Christ's name, we pray,

Amen.

Prayer for Grief

Heavenly Father,

Amid our pain and sorrow, we turn to You, the source of all comfort and hope. We lift to You all those suffering from the loss of a loved one. May Your loving presence surround them like a warm embrace, bringing peace that surpasses all understanding.

Grant them strength to endure the heaviness of their grief and may Your healing touch mend the brokenness of their hearts. Help them find comfort in their cherished memories, knowing that love transcends physical boundaries and lives on eternally.

Lord, through the darkness, we cling to the hope found in You. Help us trust in Your promise of eternal life and find the courage to face each day with renewed faith. Please help us draw closer to you during that time so we will not drift away in despair. May the light of Your love shine brightly amid our pain, guiding us towards healing and restoration.

We also pray for those who struggle to find the words to pray amidst their grief. Wrap them in Your loving arms and be their strength in times of weakness. Help them know that You are near, even when words fail.

Father, we entrust all our brokenness and pain to You, knowing that You will bring beauty from ashes. May Your grace sustain us, and Your love uphold us as we journey through the valley of grief we do not fear because we know You are with us.

We ask all things in Jesus' name,
Amen.

Prayer for Caregivers

Heavenly Father,

We come before you with hearts burdened by the challenges and responsibilities of caring for our sick loved ones. We lift all caregivers tirelessly, dedicating themselves to the well-being of those in need. Grant them the strength to endure each day's trials and the wisdom to navigate the uncertainties.

Amid the fog of life, may your light shine brightly, guiding them along the path you have laid out for them. Please help them see their role as caregivers not as a burden but as a privilege and honor bestowed upon them by your grace.

Restore their souls, O Lord, as they pour love and compassion onto others. Please give them the courage to face each day with determination and hope, knowing that you are the ultimate healer and source of comfort.

When feelings of loneliness or isolation creep in, remind them of Your constant presence and promise never to leave or forsake them. Strengthen their faith and fill their hearts with your peace that surpasses all understanding. Give them the wisdom to set time aside each day for self-care and devotion with You so You will renew them.

We pray all these things in the mighty name of Jesus,
Amen.

Lessons Learned Prayer

Father God,

Help us release any lingering anger or resentment we may hold toward You or toward those circumstances that have caused us pain. Grant us the grace to forgive and let go of bitterness and anger so peace can flood our hearts.

Forgive us for our lack of understanding and our wrong perspectives. Give us clarity and help us see things from your vantage point.

Lord, instill within us a genuine desire for healing. Fill us with hope and the determination to seek wholeness and renewal in Your loving embrace, trusting in Your divine plan for our lives.

Help us understand that faith is not contingent on receiving our desired outcome. True faith is believing that although your ways may not align with what you want, you know what is best for you.

Lord, grant us the strength to release the heavy burdens of fear and guilt that weigh upon our souls so we can grab hold of our healing.

Help us break free from these chains of grief and depression that bind us so that we can fully embrace the healing You offer.

Empower us to be intentional in choosing life, Lord. Give us the clarity of mind and the heart's resolve to actively pursue the path of healing and restoration, even amidst the darkest moments of our grief.

In Your infinite mercy and compassion, hear our earnest prayers, O Lord, and guide us on the journey of healing and restoration.

In Jesus' name, we pray,
Amen.

Divine Intercession: A Prayer for the Salvation of Souls
Most Gracious Father,

We come before you with hearts open to your divine guidance and mercy. We pray for those souls who have not yet found their way to salvation, who may be lost or wandering in darkness. Touch their hearts, Lord, with the light of your love and the truth of your Word.

Holy Spirit, we ask you to work in their lives, drawing them closer to you and opening their eyes to the beauty of your grace. Help them understand the depth of your love and the sacrifice made by your Son, Jesus Christ, for their redemption.

Grant them the courage to surrender their lives to you, confess their sins, and accept Jesus as their Lord and

Savior. May they experience the peace of knowing you and the joy of being reconciled.

We pray for divine encounters and appointments where they may encounter believers who can share the good news of salvation. Give us boldness and compassion to be your instrument in reaching out to those who are lost and need salvation.

Through Your Word, we know that salvation is a gift from You, given freely to all who believe in Jesus Christ. We lift these souls to You, those reading this book who do not know You, to have a divine encounter with You.

We are reminded of Your words in John 3:16: "For God so loved the world that he gave his one and only Son, that whoever believes in him shall not perish but have eternal life."

Romans 10:9-10: "If you declare with your mouth, 'Jesus is Lord,' and believe in your heart that God raised him from the dead, you will be saved. For it is with your heart that you believe and are justified, and it is with your mouth that you profess your faith and saved." We pray each heart whispers this declaration to you for their soul salivation.

In Jesus' name, we pray,

Amen

ACKNOWLEDGEMENTS

First and foremost, I extend my deepest gratitude to the Father, Son, and The Holy Spirit, who have been my everything. I thank You for healing my crushed heart, for being my every present help in a time of trouble, for restoring my joy, and being the guiding light that has paved the way when all seemed lost. The miracles, signs, and wonders witnessed in Sophia's life stand as a testament to Your divine grace, love, and intervention. I am profoundly thankful for the three years we were blessed to have Sophia, knowing she was given to us on loan. Thank You for knowing when to call her back so she could receive the much-needed rest she deserved.

Sophia as my heart echoes to heaven, I thank God for the time we had with you. You taught me how to be a better mother, and more importantly a better person. I learned from you the importance of being present because tomorrow is not promised to any of us. I thank you for always reminding us to pray because you knew even at 2 years old, we would need it. Thank you for being an example by showing love, compassion, and mercy to others. Because of you my faith was built, stretched, and matured. Your compacity to love, play, and laugh under so much ugliness, I stood in awe. I did not know then that I gave birth to my hero, thank you for the honor of being your mother.

I would like to express my deepest appreciation to my husband Juan Roman. Through the many storms we weathered together, you have stood beside me as a pillar of strength, a devoted father, and a BFF (best friend forever). Your steady support, heartfelt prayers, companionship, attentive ear, and love have been the steady hand that has guided us through life's challenges. I am thankful that God chose you to walk hand and hand with me.

I am forever grateful for my son Domonick Roman, (Dom), for being the lifeline God sent, the reason I got up and chose to live each day. God predestined you to be our son and I am profoundly thankful that my spirit bore witness to this truth the first time I laid eyes on you. Thank you for accepting me with an open heart, for loving me, and for granting me the privilege and honor of being your forever mommy.

Isabella Roman, (Bella), I want to express my heartfelt gratitude for being the precious gift through which God brought joy and light back into our lives. Your "smiling eyes" serve as a constant reminder to all of us to find happiness in every moment. Thank you for being the gift you are, I am blessed to be your mommy.

Estelle Mannion, (Mother), I am deeply grateful for your unconditional love and support, which has been the bedrock of my life. Mom, I am truly blessed to have your example to glean from, your guidance, love, prayers, friendship, and unwavering support to help me navigate through life. You are a pillar of strength in my life, a constant source of comfort, and I am forever grateful for you.

As a Daddy's girl, I would be remiss not to thank Thomas Mannion, my greatest fan, for loving me as you did. Dad, your unwavering support continues to inspire me, and I draw on your love to guide me even in my darkest times, despite your physical absence. I cherish the memories we shared and carry your love with me always.

I would like to express our deepest gratitude for my mother in-law, Maria Ortiz, who recently passed away. Her selfless decision to stay with us to ensure our son was taken care of during the long hospital stay will always be remembered and cherished.

I am immensely grateful to Bishop Dwayne and Pastor Tracey Meyers for their steadfast leadership over the past five years. Under your guidance, healing has blossomed in every facet of my life.

I am deeply grateful to my brother-in-law, Leonardo (Wise) Roman, for consistently suggesting that I turn my journal into a book. Thank you for allowing God to use you.

We appreciate our sister-friend Jenice Green for allowing God to use prophetic dreaming to warn and prepare us, anchoring our emotions during a frightening time.

I want to acknowledge my Cousin Jeanna McKnight for being our rock and stepping up to aid us in the details of our daughter's funeral. God truly used you, Danielle Chase, and my mother, to prevent me from falling apart.

I want to express my gratitude to our brothers and sisters who worked alongside us in ministry while in New York. Even though our paths may have led us in different directions, I will always remember the love and friendship you have shown us during the countless trials we endured.

I want to thank Genesis, one of Sophia's BFF for honoring her memory recently after all these years by dedicating a lip-gloss collection in her honor titled "Baby

Sophia." You can support her Instagram @Pieces0fhope. Sophia cherished her time with you & David.

I would like to express my heartfelt gratitude to Ruth Huffman, CEO of the American Childhood Cancer Organization, for granting me the opportunity to utilize my experiences as a former board member to make a difference, and for her decision to honor our daughter's memory by including her in the preface of a book assisting families dealing with a rare form of brain cancer.

To all our beloved family, friends, and supporters - During the most trying period of our lives, your support has been oxygen. Your prayers, words of comfort, and tangible acts of love have helped us stand through the storm. Your kindness and steadfast support have truly been a stabilizing force in our lives. I am profoundly grateful for your presence in our lives and for the invaluable role you have played in allowing God's blessings to flow through you. Your generosity and compassion have made a world of difference, and I will forever cherish the impact you have had on our lives.

Thank you to all the unknown individuals who prayed for us. Your selfless acts of kindness and intercession have brought comfort and strength during our difficult times, and for that, we are grateful. I would like to thank Denise and Kiana Dancie for their invaluable help during this process.

With heartfelt love and gratitude to all!

ABOUT THE AUTHOR

As a devout servant of God and advocate for positive change, Dr. Nicole Estelle Roman has proudly worn many hats throughout her journey. As an Elder Designate, Marketing and Business Consultant, and Master Coach, she is dedicated to serving both divine purpose and human betterment. She has served on numerous boards, including the American Childhood Cancer Organization, where she's contributed to vital discussions and initiatives.

To empower the next generation, Dr. Roman has mentored young adults and spearheaded various programs aimed at enriching educational experiences within the community. Her dedication to service has been recognized with the prestigious Presidential Lifetime Award for Volunteerism, a testament to her unwavering commitment to uplifting others and inspiring them to embrace their fullest potential.

www.ingramcontent.com/pod-product-compliance
Lightning Source LLC
Chambersburg PA
CBHW070054080526
44586CB00013B/1059